**Mel Bay's**

# COMPLETE CLAWHAMMER BANJO BOOK

## by Lisa Schmitz & Alec Slater

© 2008, 1994 BY MEL BAY PUBLICATIONS, INC., PACIFIC, MO 63069.

**Visit us on the Web at www.melbay.com — E-mail us at email@melbay.com**

# CONTENTS

# DEDICATION

To the guiding spirit who showed me what it was like to be played by a banjo in the first place.

# FOREWORD

This manual is intended for the clawhammer-frailing banjo player with some experience in this style already. Although not an instruction manual per se, some of the basics of the style have been included. These are intended as review only and should not take the place of a qualified teacher. This traditional style of playing can really only fully be learned from the living oral tradition it has grown in. I strongly urge anyone wanting to get this playing "right" to find someone in your area who plays and have him/her teach you. Listen to it, watch it, and make it your own.

Some of the tunes here are quite simple and can be easily picked up by the less experienced player. Overall I have striven for simplicity in rendering these tunes. Therein I feel lies the beauty of clawhammer banjo.

Alec Slater

# INTRODUCTION

## PART 1

### A. History

So here I am presenting a book of Irish and Irish-derived music, to be played on an instrument of African origin, in a style essentially coming from the Southern Appalachian Mountains of the U.S. How did we get here?

The black people of Western Africa were taken into boats to become slaves for the Southern white plantation owners of America in the 1700s. Fortunately they took with them in their heads the remembrance of an instrument dominant in their culture at the time. It was basically a large hollow gourd covered with an animal hide. Attached to the gourd was a stick from which gut strings were connected. This served as the basic model for the banjo in these early days. Eventually the instrument, then made of wood, fell into the hands of the poorer white Southern people and gained much popularity. In the early 1800s a man named Joel Walker Sweeney apparently added a short small fifth string above the bass string, to be used as a drone, and thus created the five-string banjo.

The banjo's popularity waxed and waned for many years through this country. It even went west with the covered wagons in the late 1800s. But its stronghold was always with the mountain people of the Southern Appalachians, as it is to this day. The style of clawhammer, also commonly called "frailing," was developed and used in the Southern Appalachians. Many other styles of playing were also used, such as up picking, two-finger picking and three-finger Scruggs-style picking. The frailing style is considered to be the most ancient, preceding the others in development. The actual origin of frailing or clawhammer style are today shrouded in mystery.

The material that came to be played on the banjo in this style came from the musical traditions of the people who played it. When the settlers from the British Isles came to America, they brought with them their fiddles and a rich and extensive collection of tunes. The reels, jigs, waltzes, hornpipes and dance tunes of these people were integrated into the developing music and style of the time.

Here in a sense was a "melting pot" of style, instrument, and song.

### B. Purpose and Intentions

After having played in the Southern Appalachian tradition of old-time banjo playing for a while, I became aware that many other types of tunes fit the style quite well. Of late I have been going through this old-time style of music to its roots in the British Isles. I have found many tunes which in essence "missed the boat" and didn't make it over with the settlers to become part of that old-time repertoire. I have been pleased to find, especially in the Irish tradition, much music which fits this style perfectly.

Most of the material here has not often been heard played on the banjo in this way. Thus I hope to be breathing new life into clawhammer banjo picking, showing specifically ways in which the style may be adapted to fit these tunes. There are melodic limits to this style, I'll admit. Hopefully this book will inspire you to realize that most of the limits are really only in your mind. These limits can easily be overcome through the graceful selection of important melody notes within each piece.

The music of the Southern Appalachians and also of the British Isles are highly modal in character. To me this is one of the attractive beauties of it—it is that lonesome, sometimes airy, ancient-sounding quality that so often strikes our heart's chords. I feel the material I have presented here should broaden and deepen your appreciation for modal music, in both theory and playing possibilities.

# PART 2

## Scales, Modal Structure, and Banjo Tunings

A brief explanation into the structure of the scales used in this music is important only in an academic sense. Certainly it is not necessary to know this in order to enjoy and play the music. For those who enjoy theory and remain somewhat baffled by what a mode is, I hope the following will enlighten.

---

A mode I'll define as the structure or relationship of notes or tones within a scale. There are many ways a scale may be structured with the tones at hand.

If you have a piano there in front of you, play all the white keys from C to C. The notes are: C D E F G A B C. The distance from E to F, and also from B to C is a half step (or one fret on the banjo). The distance between all the other notes are whole steps.

C—D—E⌢F—G—A—B⌢C

whole whole  half  whole whole whole half

Play this scale a number of times and remember how it sounds. This is our major scale or mode of today. It is also called the Ionian mode.

To play the banjo in the Ionian mode, or major mode, the most common tunings used are:

Key of G-  g D G B D -   (the small "g" here represents the short fifth string of the banjo, then fourth, third, etc.)

Key of A-  a E A C♯ E -   this is basically the same as above only tuned up, or capoed up two frets, a whole tone.

Key of A-  a D A D E  or a D A D F♯

Key of C-  g C G C D

---

A mode may be played in any key as long as the relationships of the half and whole steps remain the same. Key may be defined as the note which usually starts or ends the tune (though not always), and is the main tone that the tune revolves around. Thus the scale shown above is the C major or Ionian scale. To play in G major while preserving the same relationships of the basic scale we must use an F♯:

G A B⌢C D E F♯⌢G

half           half

We see here that in the major scale the half steps occur between the 3rd and 4th, and 7th and 8th notes or degrees of the scale.

A D major scale would be: D E F♯ G A B C♯ D; and an A major: A B C♯ D E F♯ G♯ A.

---

By the use of the sharps and flats (accidentals) the pitch may be raised or lowered to fit the pattern of each particular mode or scale.

Now play all the white keys starting from D to D: D E F G A B C D. We see here the half steps occur between the 2nd and 3rd and also the 6th and 7th degrees of the scale. This is the Dorian mode.

Many old-time fiddle tunes are in this beautiful airy-sounding mode. The banjo, to play in this mode easily, uses the mountain minor or sawmill tuning. Usually pitched in the key of A or G this would be: g D G C D, or tuned up a whole tone or capoed up two frets for the key of A: a E A D E. As you can see, the only difference between the G major tuning and the sawmill tuning is the second string raised up a half (½) step, i.e.:

g D G B D major G
g D G C D mountain minor G

---

Playing all the white keys on your piano from A to A — A B C D E F G A — will give you the modern-day minor scale or Aeolian mode. Play it a few times, then play the major scale to hear the difference in feeling. As you can see, this A minor scale uses all the same notes as the C major scale, just arranged differently. Thus the relative minor key of C major is said to be A. Using the pattern above for the minor scale, figure out what notes would be in an E minor scale, the find out what its relative major key is.

(Answer)    (E F♯ G A B C D E - Relative major: G)

---

The last mode I'll talk about here is the Myxolydian mode. Using all white keys it goes from G to G:  G A B C D E F G.

As you can see in the pattern of half steps, the first four notes are in the same pattern as the first four notes of the major scale. That is: a half step between the 3rd and 4th degrees, thus making this mode very major sounding. The last four notes of the scale, however, differ in that the half step is between the 6th and 7th notes rather than the 7th and 8th as in the major scale. An A Myxolydian scale would be A B C♯ D E F♯ G A.

---

The banjo tunings already given above work just as well for these last two modes. The minor mode fits the sawmill tuning well, also the aDADE tuning. The Myxolydian is easily fit to either major or minor tunings. A nice D minor tuning to try sometime is: aDADF, or G minor gDGB♭D. The point of all these tunings is to try and get as many open strings as possible to be the essential notes within each key and mode. In making up new tunings you are limited only by your imagination and relative frustration of having to retune all the time.

The other three modes, rarely, if ever, used these days are the Phrygian mode (from E → E), the Lydian mode (F → F), and the Locrian (B → B).

---

The banjo grew up playing music which used many different modes. Irish and old-time Appalachian music is very modal in character. To accommodate all these different modes, while maintaining a relatively simple way of playing a tune, the strings of the banjo were tuned in many different ways. Over fifty different types of banjo tunings have been collected. This book concentrates on only about three of the major tunings used today.

# PART 3

## Use of Tablature and Clawhammer Movements . . . . a review

Tablature is a written form of shorthand for the stringed instrument player. It shows the mechanics of rendering a particular piece of music, i.e.: what fret to play, or with what finger, as well as timing and other movements. What it does not and cannot do is to let you **hear** what the piece **sounds** like. Unfortunately we are using a written-visual medium to communicate a vibrational-hearing experience. So really there is a great deal lacking in learning this way, but it is not without its merits. The use of tablature must be properly balanced with hearing how a tune **sounds** when played. It should be used to merely show one way of playing a tune and to help find where the notes are and how they may be played. Once you can get that far, then **close the book** and really play the music with all the individual inspirations and subtleties you can muster. By no means should you play it every time as written here, or try to memorize exactly how it "should" be played. There are many ways to learn music—from books, tablature, records, friends —but the most important thing to do is listen, and hear.

In tablature we have five lines that represent each string of the banjo. The bottom line is the short fifth string, the top line is the first string. A letter is written on each line showing what note that string is to be tuned to:

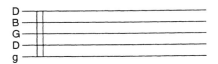

A number is written on top of a line and this shows what fret number to press. An "O" means the string is to be played open, or unfretted. Chords are shown as two or more strings played simultaneously:

The index finger plays the note marked "I" below the tab. This is done by knocking the string down with the fingernail in the traditional frailing manner.

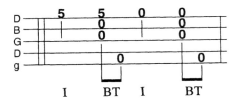

"B T" below the tab indicates the typical brushing of a chord and thumb note on the fifth string, sequence. For simplicity I have left out these letter notes below the tab unless further clarification is needed. This should make tablature reading easier.

Hammer-ons are indicated this way:

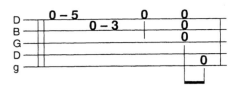

And are noted with an "H" below the tab only where needed, showing the note hammered on to:

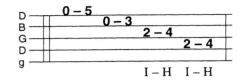

Sliding notes are indicated in this manner, with an "SL" below the tab showing the note to be slid to:

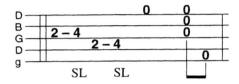

A pull-off is shown as:

And again, is indicated with a "P" only where further clarity is needed.

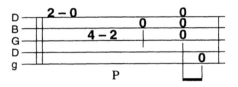

The basic clawhammer-style lick is to pick a string down with the index finger and follow it quickly with a thumbed note on one of the strings below it. This is shown in tablature as:

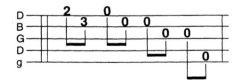

I will only include notes below the tab when needed. It should be assumed that this is played with the right-hand fingers like this:

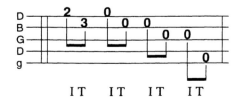

Any questions to my use of tablature, or with any tune here will be gladly answered.

# Being Played

It sat down to play me
Placing itself snugly on my lap.


My belly, the gut skin of its ancient past
While strings vibrate the lonely joyous cavities of my heart
and intricacies of delicate pattern
     dance in my mind's eye.


"Dance" it shouted, "move in the worlds
     of jubilation and utter infant delight"
"and cry too," to share the joy with sorrow and pain
     and balance the constellation of being.


"Who is playing who?" I asked
     "and which of us is really being tuned here?"


While breathing rhythm and melody of earth, water, fire and air
     in and out, over and again
It seemed to not even care of these questions,
     as if to say,
"you know already the answer in your heart."


"Play me," it said
     "But then be played by me."


—Alec Slater 10/78

# IRISH TUNES

# PLANXTY GEORGE BRABIZON

A beautiful tune supposedly composed by the famous Irish harper Turlough O'Carolan. "Planxty" is an Irish word meaning basically: "in honor of," or "dedicated to." Thus the song is in honor of George Brabizon, whoever he was. Recently I have heard the tune called "Twa Bonnie Maidens" and sung. The words tell the story of Bonnie Prince Charlie's flight to the Isle of Skye during the 1745 Rebellion. Either way it's a fine piece that I prefer to play relatively slowly. Goes great with whistles and concertinas.

Take special care with the B part on the first and second measures. The "R" indicates a roll. The index finger strikes down on the second then first string for the total time of an eighth note, then the thumb catches the fifth string for the first beat of the next measure. The rolled notes should sound separate and distinct. This technique is similar to the "Galax Lick."

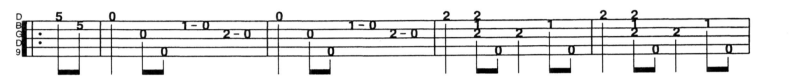

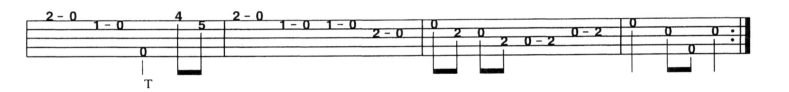

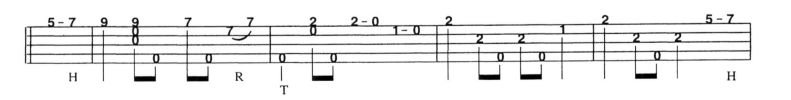

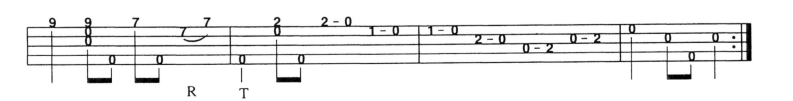

# THE FLOWERS OF EDINBURGH

# SCOTLAND THE BRAVE

That old favorite brought back to life, if indeed it was ever dead. An example of how the clawhammer style and the music of the British Isles go together so well. The fit here between melodic line and limits of style is perfect.

In measure B³ the high G chord is obtained thusly. Also in that measure use the pinky to get the 10th fret note there as the other three fingers make the chord. In the next measure use the ring finger to fret the 2nd string at the 9th fret.

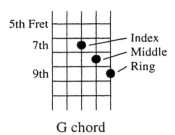

G chord

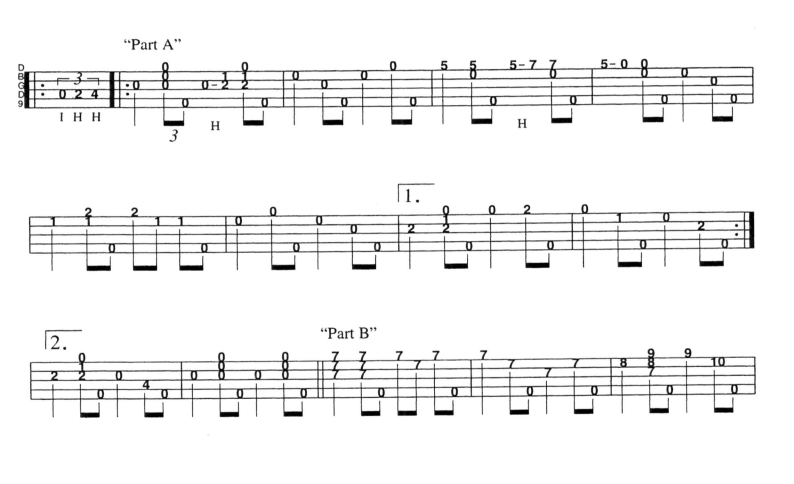

Then play part A with second ending, then start from part A again.

# MORPETH'S HORN PIPE or MORPETH'S RANT

Note in the 2nd measure a new way to produce a triplet, the staple (or one of them!) of Irish music. Play this tune quickly but clearly. A rant has nothing to do with a rage or a rave (I don't think) but is a type of dance. A great pennywhistle tune.

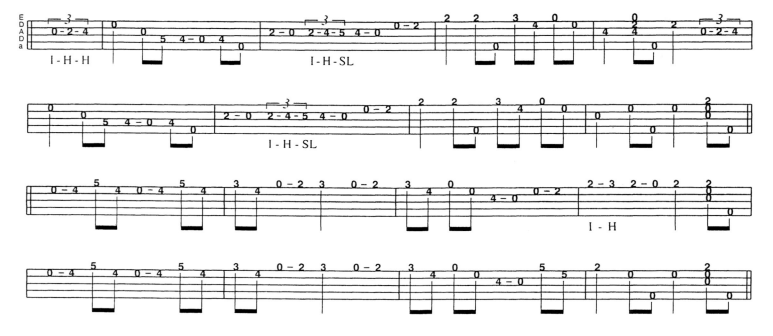

# THE MORNING STAR

In part A, measure 4, the F# (4th fret on the bass string) could be obtained with the thumb, but it is vastly easier to hammer on with the left hand's ring finger. In part B, measure 3, use the index finger to hammer to the D note (3rd fret-2nd string)—then barre at the 5th fret to get that C chord. By then sliding the barre up to the 7th fret the next configuration can be easily obtained.

measure B7 Variaton:                                                              etc. end

14

# OFF TO CALIFORNIA

This is a hard tune to play with the right feeling and bounce put into it. Note the triplets that occur; these are three notes to be quickly played within the space of one beat. They are obtained by first hitting the open bass string with the right-hand index finger, then quickly hammer on to the second fret, and then the fourth. On the left hand the index finger and ring finger are best to use for the hammers. This is a common movement in Irish clawhammer banjo.

Also note the transition from measure two to three in part A. Here the thumb note is struck on the downbeat or first beat of measure three. The trick to doing this smoothly is to keep the thumb on the fifth string, resting, ready, and waiting while you're doing the immediately preceding hammer-on of the first string. Then as your foot comes down for that first beat, cock your hand back and thumb the fifth string. A little patience and close attention to the tablature will get it just right.

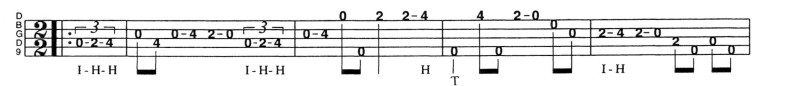

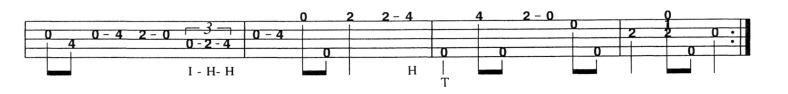

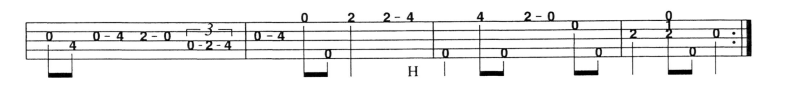

# STATEN ISLAND HORNPIPE

That's a C chord in part B; it gives this tune a lovely taste of the Myxolydian mode in an otherwise major mode piece. Try starting out part B with a roll from time to time to really keep this piece moving along.

Variant: measure A4

# SPEED THE PLOW

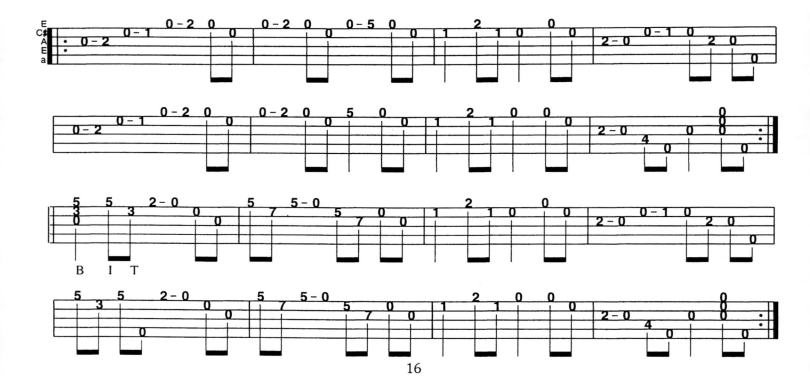

# DEVIL'S DREAM

Surprised to see this one here? It didn't come easy to turn this fine fiddle tune into a clawhammer banjo piece. Though usually played at breakneck speeds in a 3-finger style of banjo picking, the piece here must, of necessity, go a bit slower. So try to find a fiddler who knows this one and do what you can to get her or him to slow it down, then listen carefully so you can hear all the fullness of the tune. If a devil dreamed up this one I'd love to hear one played from an angel's dream sometime, heavenly.

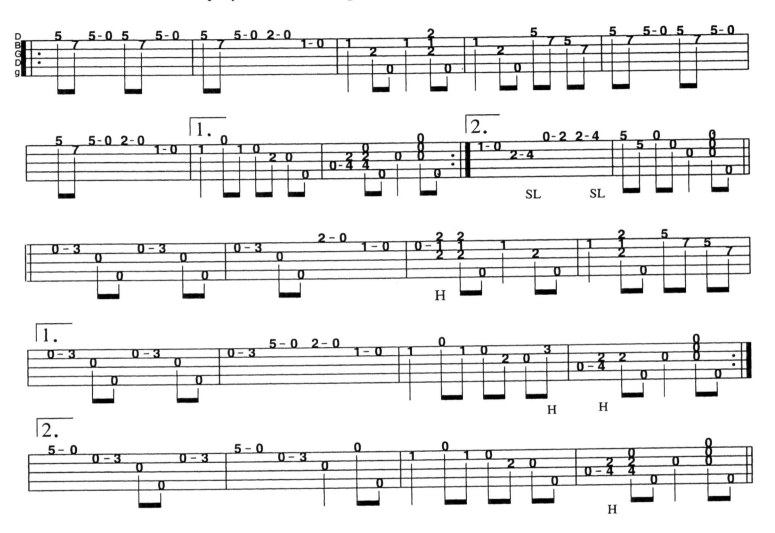

Play part A, then part B, then part A with the variations described below:

Substitute measures $A^1$ and $A^2$ for:

and measures $A^5$ and $A^6$ with:

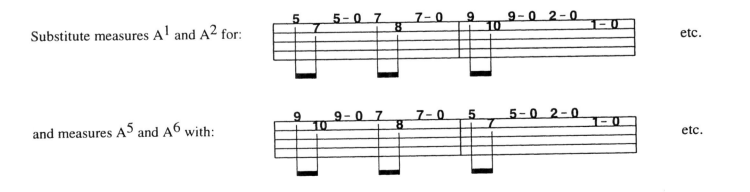

etc.

etc.

# RAKISH PADDY

A strange old Irish modal tune that moves quite fast. I learned to play it in medley form with "Soldier's Joy" from some musician friends near Chico, California.

One of the other ways to produce a triplet is shown here, in the third measure of the second part. While fingering the first string at the third fret with the index finger, quickly hammer with the ring finger to the fifth fret, then quickly pull off back to the third fret from the fifth. This should be done very quickly.

# SAILOR'S HORNPIPE

Traditionally, hornpipes are played quite slowly, much slower than reels though both are in 4/4 or 2/2 time. This is a very difficult tune for clawhammer banjo to play soft, smooth and flowing. Go slow. The chord that is being worked around in the 3rd measure of part B is an A minor chord (A, C, E) and is made this way:

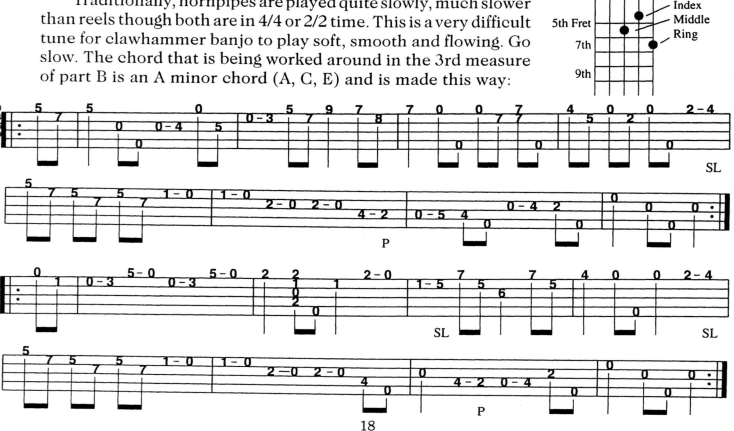

# LADY MONTGOMERY

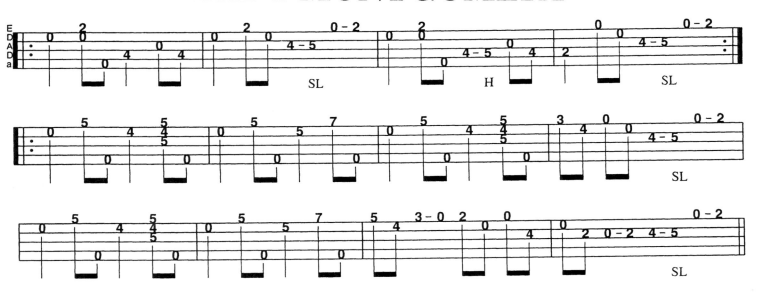

# FAREWELL TO WHISKEY

I'd like to hear the inebriated banjo player (who told me that to be a REAL banjo picker I'd have to start drinking whiskey) play this fond farewell. Play it as a soft, slow, sad song with tenderness in its parting melody.

In the 4th measure of part A use the pinky to hammer on to the 3rd fret-2nd string while making the E minor chord.

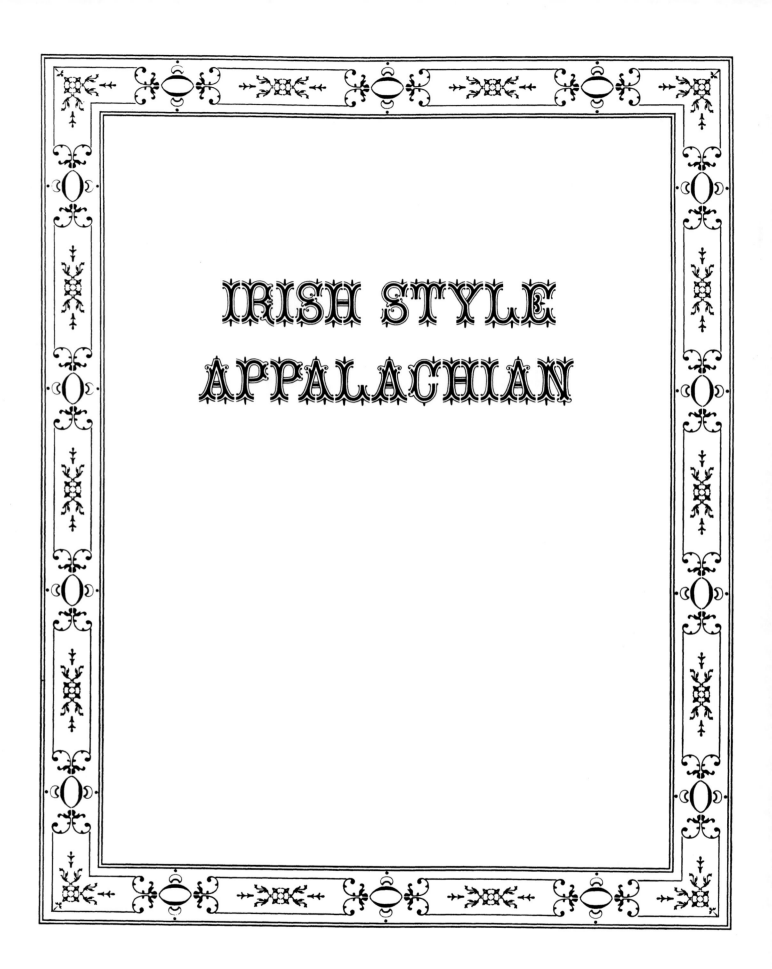

# IRISH STYLE
# APPALACHIAN

# BONAPARTE CROSSING THE RHINE

This is the more familiar old-time version. Listen to the Fuzzy Mountain String Band's version. It goes not too fast but with lots of strong feelings behind it. One of my favorites.

Note in third measure of part A where the thumbed note is actually a whole separate note, and not just thrown in for effect. It is an important melody note, and deserves emphasis. Be sure to keep the timing correct here. Refer to the variant noted below for another way of doing this measure. This is a good technique for utilizing the full potential of the fifth string in clawhammer banjo and giving the melody line an interesting little punctuation mark.

Then to part A played with second ending, then from beginning again.

Variation measure A[4]:

21

# OLD BILL CHEATHUM

Alternate A part

# THE BETHEL STREET REEL

An original composition, dedicated to my old home on Bethel Drive across from the railroad switching yards.

# WEISER TUNE

All those double notes in part A require careful thumb work so it doesn't sound too muddy. The triplets are of the double hammer variety and are indicated with a line and a (3) over the notes.

This version came from the Weiser, Idaho, Fiddle Festival held the third week of June every year near the Snake River.

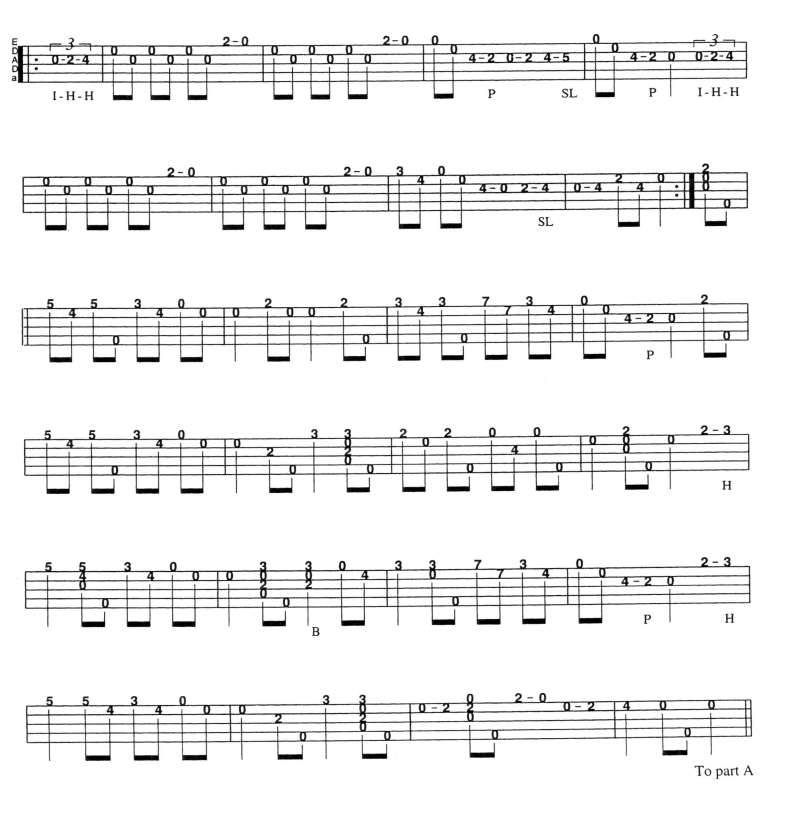

To part A

# BANJO SHUFFLE

Note that part B has ten measures instead of the usual eight. The third measure of part B is tricky with that thumbed note. Be sure it gets played with the proper emphasis and time. Instead of that thumb string you could get the same note on the fifth fret of the first string.

Try measure A³ this way too:

# TURKEY IN THE STRAW

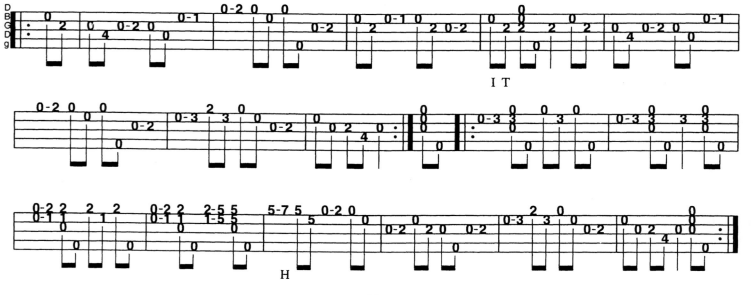

# SLATER'S HORNPIPE

The trickiest part here is in part B, measure four. The R is a roll, produced by barring at the seventh fret and moving the index finger from the second to first string in a "choppy" sort of way and then flicking the fifth string with the thumb. Refer to the "*" for a more conventional, though harder, way of doing this to get the timing correct.

Part A measure seven: the last note in the measure there is produced by hammering on HARD to the open bass string on the fourth fret to produce the note F#, rather than trying to get it with the thumb.

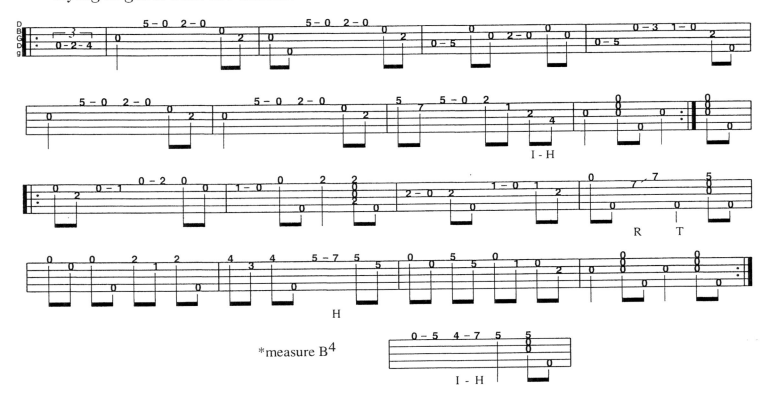

*measure B⁴

# FORKED DEER

# IRISH MODAL

# STAR OF THE COUNTY DOWN

In A minor, also see the waltz version of this fine tune later in the book. The two go great played together as a medley. There are melodic similarities here also with "Bonaparte Crossing the Rhine."

Each part is played once. Note in the 5th measure of part A where the 3rd string is hammered on to the 2nd fret although it has not been struck by the right hand. You have to hammer on hard enough to sound the note here.

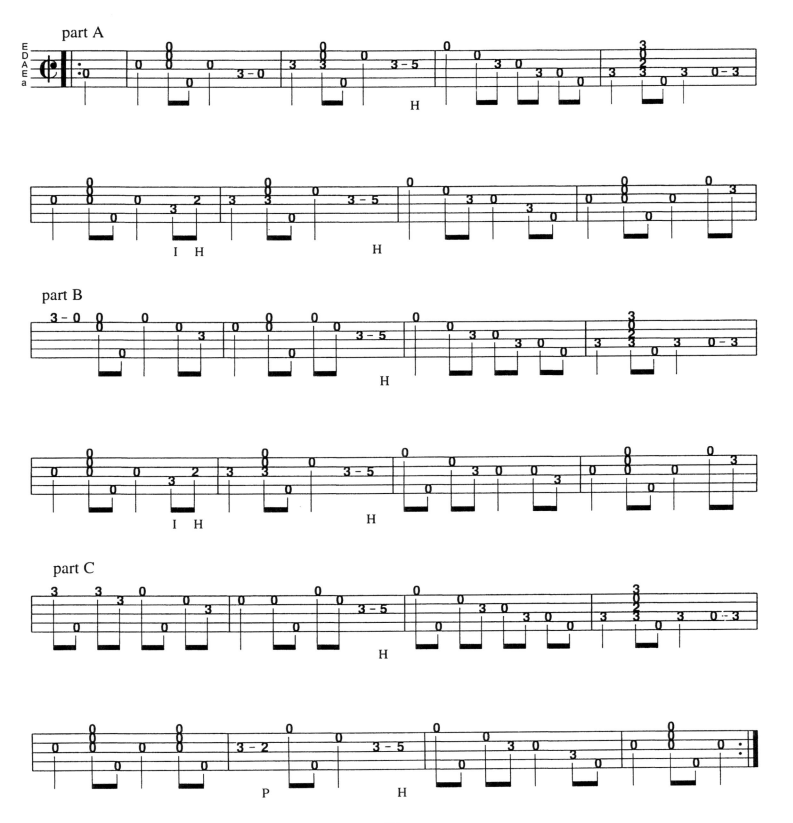

# JENNY PICKING COCKLES

Though tuned in the G mountain minor tuning, the song is in the Myxolydian mode in the key of D. Some strangely beautiful harmonies result.

At the point (*) noted in measure two, continue to keep the string fretted after striking the note so that it can be heard while the other notes in the measure are being played.

# THE MUSICAL PRIEST

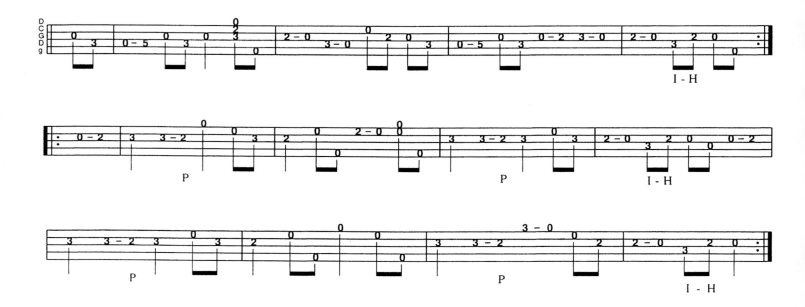

# THE HIGHWAY TO LIMERICK

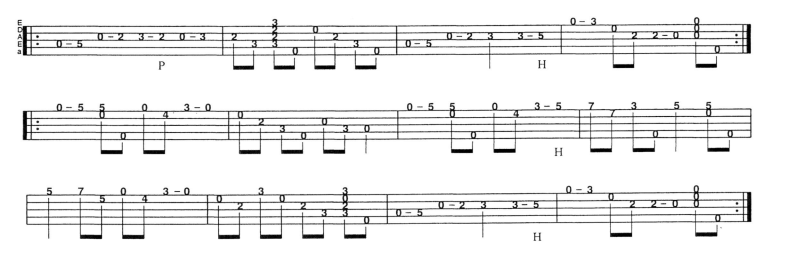

# FROST AND SNOW

Note the tuning carefully—it's a strange one! This is the only way I could figure to play this song and have all the notes in a somewhat easy playing sequence. We're in the Dorian mode here in the key of A (using a G major scale). This is a good example of how the banjo can be retuned to fit the song, so it can be played with greater facility. Two chords that I've figured out in this tuning are shown below. The fifth string tuned to the high A here doesn't always sound so good when played in certain parts, so strike it more lightly than you normally would.

Put on your warm woollies to play this one!

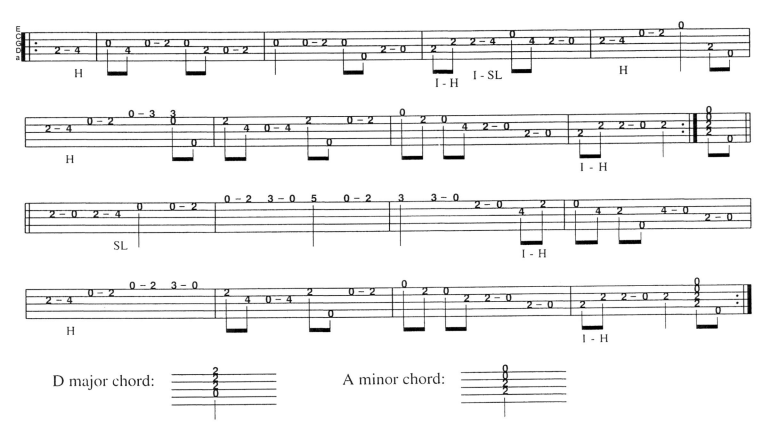

D major chord:

A minor chord:

29

# THE FIRST OF MAY

This song seems hardly reminiscent of May or flowers or birds singing to me. Maybe it speaks of love, not yet found, but long yearned for. In A minor (Aeolian).

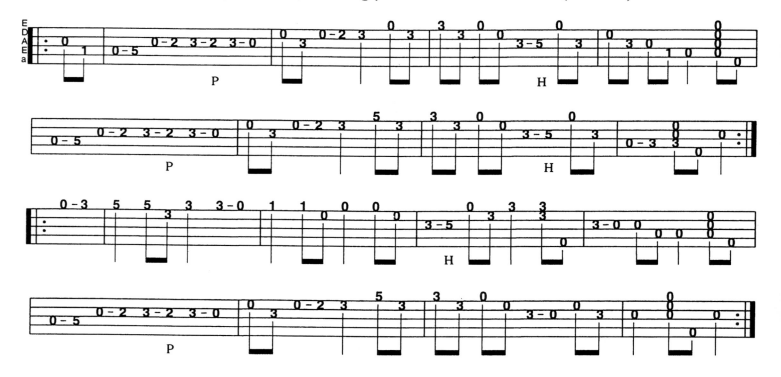

# BONAPARTE CROSSING THE RHINE

A tune by the same name also exists in the key of D. It is not a modal tune, however. The melody is very different. Refer to the recording by the Fuzzy Mountain String Band for that version.

The most difficult phrase here is the second measure of part A. Leave the index finger on the third fret of the third string. Then using the ring or little finger, **quickly** hammer to the fifth fret. The first measure of part B is similar. Use your second finger to slide with here, then you can use your index finger to hammer on the first string.

# DROWSY MAGGY

Though played in the key of E minor, the banjo here is tuned in the open A tuning. I tried to figure this tune out in a D minor tuning like: aDADE capoed up to E, and also in a G tuning (the relative major of E minor), but the version here worked out to be the simplest and most beautiful.

As this tune so nicely and evenly passes from one part to the other almost by surprise, it is impossible to end. Therefore, after tiring with it, simply brush the E[7] chord as shown for resolution.

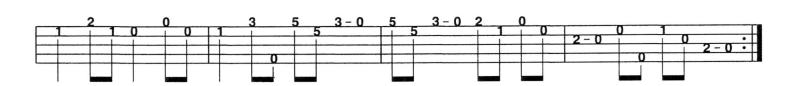

end with:

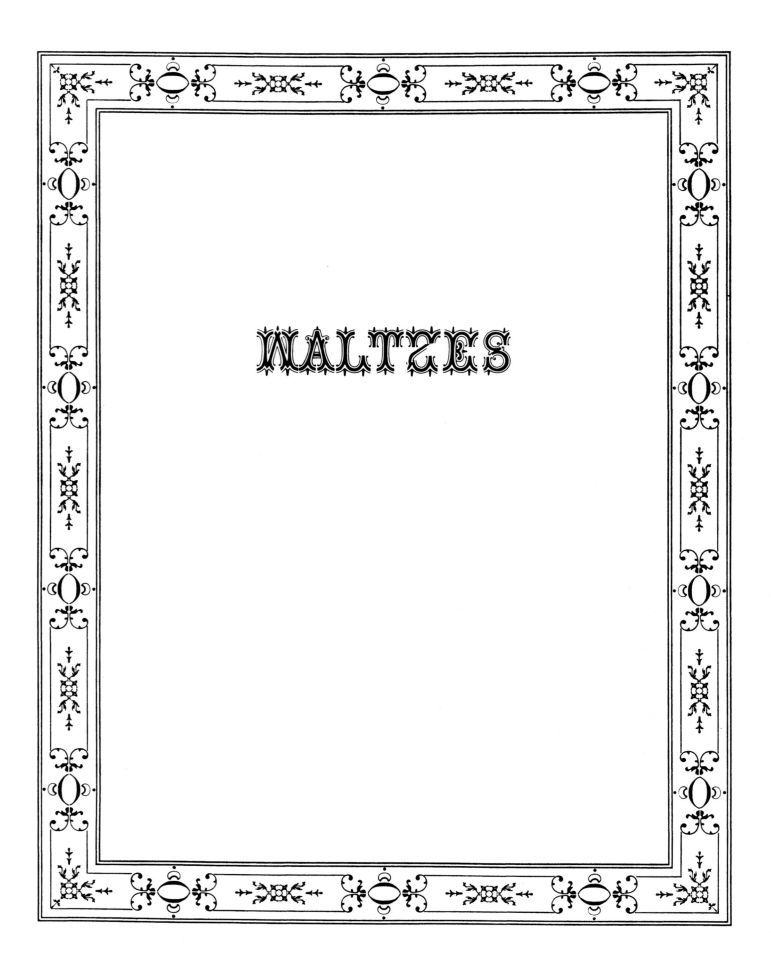

# WALTZES

# OH, COME YE TO ZION

An old well-known church song adapted many years ago from the Welsh melody called "The Ashgrove." Work at getting a lyrical flowing smoothness to it. The words are from The Old Testament; Jeremiah 31:12.

     —Therefore they shall come, and sing in the height of Zion.
        and shall flow together, to the goodness of the Lord.
     —For wheat and for wine, and oil and for the young
        the young of the flock, and of the herd.
     —And their soul shall be, as a watered garden
        and they shall not sorrow, anymore at all.

# DERMOT O'DOWD

A 3/4 time piece by the famous Irish harper O'Carolan.

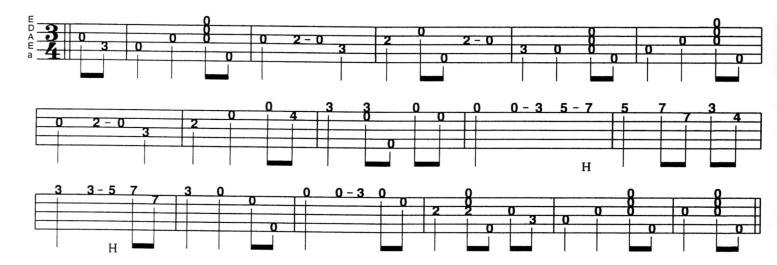

# SHE'S LIKE THE SWALLOW

The first version uses a D minor tuning, aDADF. The second version is set in the usual aDADE tuning.

# WALTZING OVER THE WATERFALL

This is a reworking of that great old-time tune, done in a waltz-time version. Pay particular attention to where the downbeats are, at the beginning of each measure, and be sure to accent these the most.

In my opinion there's not enough tunes played in waltz style on the old-time banjo. It's a whole area of playing that most pickers have totally neglected. These tunes should show some possibilities in this area.

35

# COUNTY DOWN WALTZ

This time we see this tune in 3/4 or waltz time played somewhat slow on a warm star-filled night. This version was inspired by Bill Spence's hammer dulcimer playing. The slash marks represent the half-way points of each part.

The second time through part B
substitute these measures:

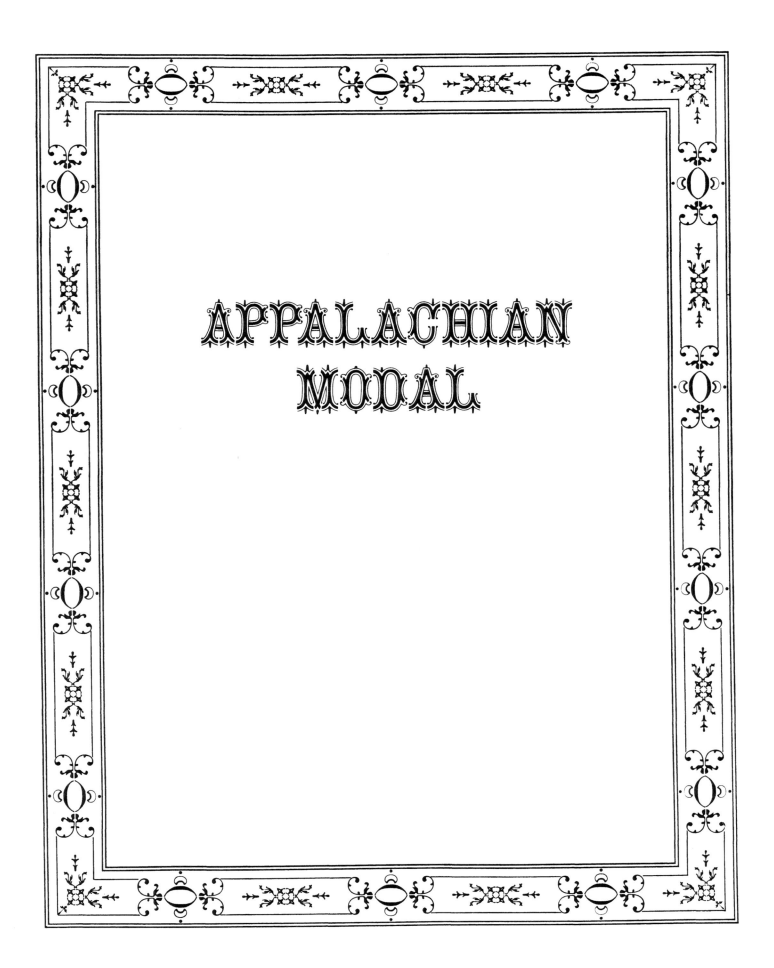

# APPALACHIAN MODAL

# CONSOLATION

## COME LIFE, SHAKER LIFE

An old song from the Shaker tradition, the people who gave us all "Tis a gift to be simple."

> Come Life, Shaker Life, Come Life eternal
> Shake, Shake it out of me, all that is carnal
>
> I'll take nimble steps, I'll be a David
> I'll show Michael twice how he behaved.

In the key of E minor, using the relative major, G, to tune the banjo.

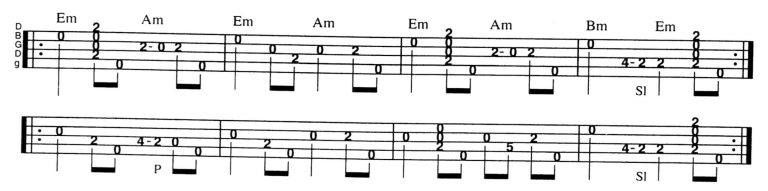

# LINCOLN STREET BLUES

Learned on Lincoln Street. In a G minor tuning, the second string is a B♭. When fretted at the 4th fret it should sound the same as the first string played open. A beautiful tune for a beautiful tuning.

39

# GIVE THE FIDDLER A DRAM

In the third measure of part B the fifth fret is barred across with the index finger and then slid up to the seventh fret barred.

Words to the first part:    Fiddler's Dram, Fiddler's Dram
Dance all night with a bottle in his hand
Bottle in his hand, Bottle in his hand
Dance all night, give the fiddler a dram.

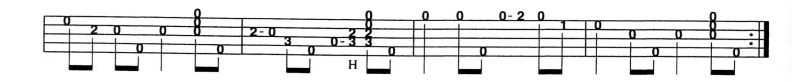

# SANTA ANA'S RETREAT

Santa Ana was the Mexican general involved in the Battle of the Alamo way back when in Texas. The origin of this tune, however, is unknown to me.

In the variants shown for part A, measure one and five, the thumbed note on the fifth string is to be sounded as if it were a separate note, receiving a full one-half beat. You can get an idea of how it should sound, time-wise, by playing the regular version first.

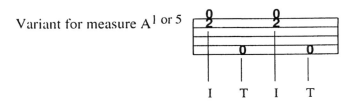

Variant for measure A¹ or 5

41

# KIOWA SPECIAL

I learned this beautiful modal piece from a friend in Chico, California, and haven't ever heard of anyone else who knew this piece. Probably the title refers to a train; it certainly has that lonesome train sound to the first part. The second part is purely major sounding and may be varied melodically to no end.

Try adding the variation that I've noted below. The timing is a bit unusual in that one. Each grouping shown receives one beat. The first note of each group is sounded on the down beat, and each note should be sounded for approximately the same length of time. Careful thumb control is needed to make it sound nice.

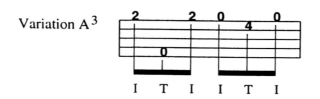

Variation A

42

# EAST VIRGINIA

The first modal banjo tune I ever learned.

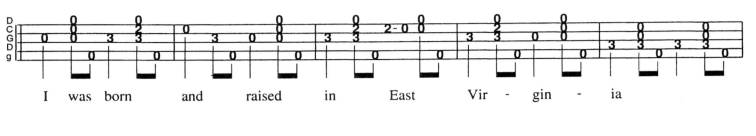

I was born and raised in East Vir - gin - ia

To North Caro - lin - a I did go.

# SALLY IN THE GARDEN

There's a beautiful version of this tune in the aDADE tuning, although it's a slightly different rendition. I've tabbed it out here pretty simply; this is mostly how I play it on the fretless banjo. Its rhythmic structure makes it very easy to add any spontaneous figures that may come to your fingers, keeping in mind of course that the simplicity of the tune is beauty itself.

# WEST VIRGINIA GALS

Another great old-time fretless banjo tune. Play part A twice through, part B three times, and part C twice.

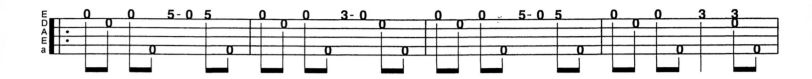

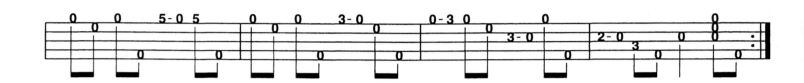

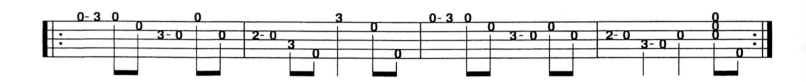

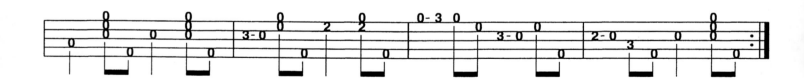

# NINE HUNDRED MILES

# TATER PATCH

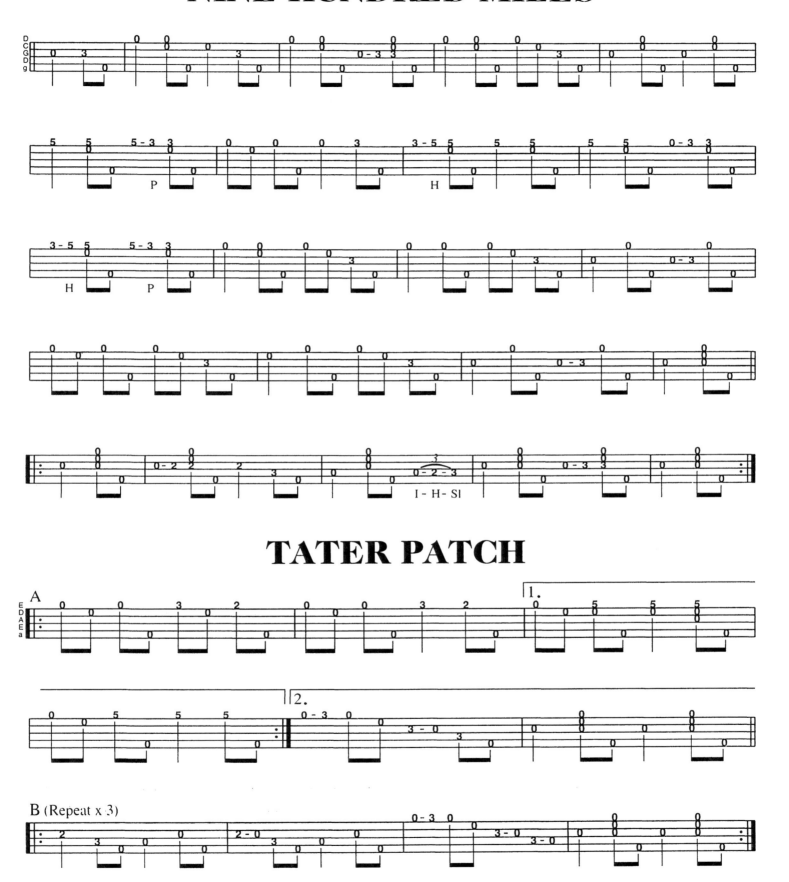

# PRETTY POLLY

"Pretty Polly" was the original tune, then Woody Guthrie took it and changed it around a little, added some wonderful verses, and "Pastures of Plenty," a song of migrant workers, was born.

This version is my own arrangement of all the ways I've ever heard "Pretty Polly" and "Pastures of Plenty," all rolled into one. The folk process continues!

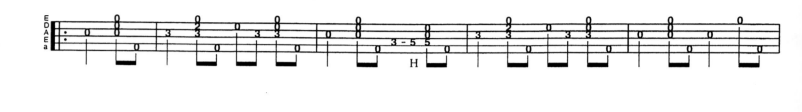

# SHADY GROVE

This wonderful old standby is a modal tune almost everyone knows. I've tabbed it out here in numerous different ways.

On this page are included the first part, the most familiar, and then a "B" part learned at the Weiser, Idaho, Fiddle Festival some years back. The last two lines show the "A" part played up the neck a whole octave up, sometimes difficult in this style.

On the next page is the same song, only worked out in an old-time two-finger picking style which I sometimes play it in.

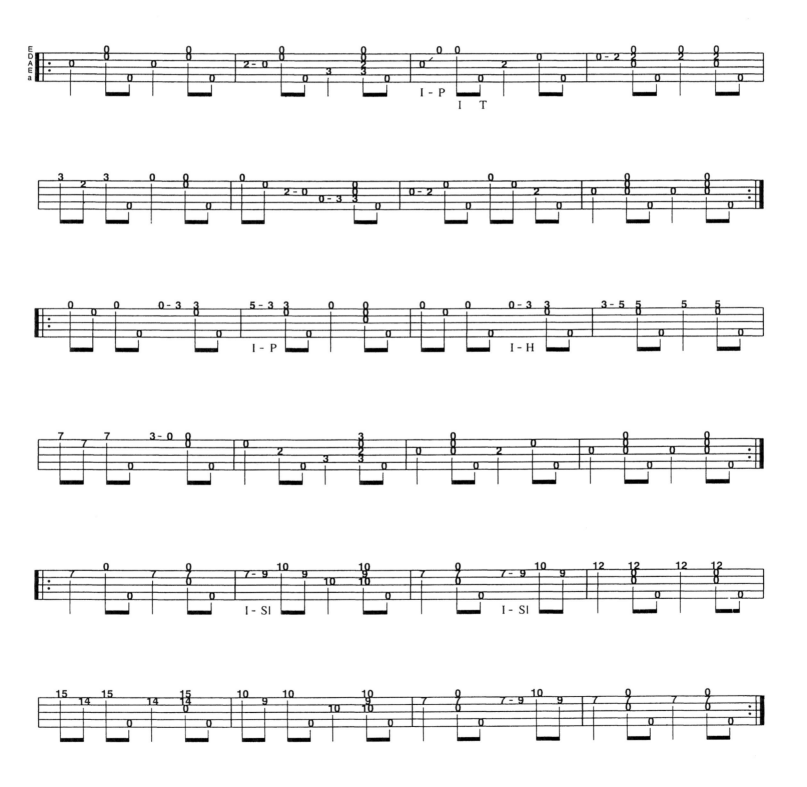

# SHADY GROVE

Two-finger picking style, the lines above the measures show the main important melody notes of the tune. Learn the easy clawhammer version first.

I have shown letters underneath the notes for the right-hand movements. The strings are picked up rather than clawhammer style. Try going from one style to the next mid-stream. In mountain minor tuning.

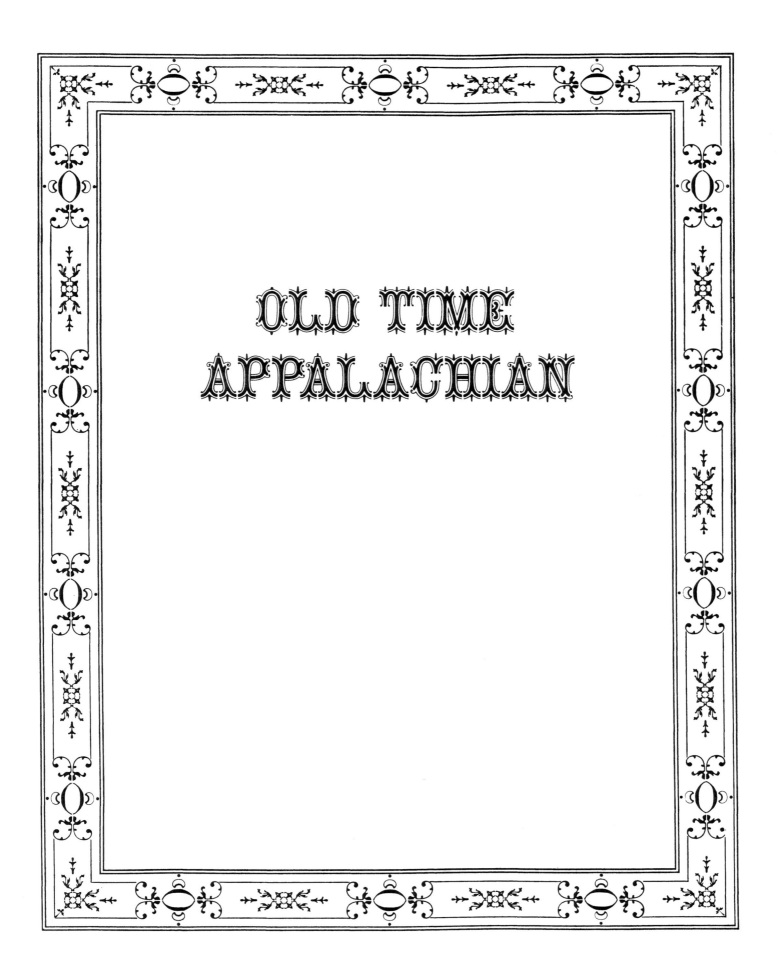

# OLD TIME APPALACHIAN

# SOMETIMES I DRINK WHISKEY

Learned this one from a fiddler friend named Stuart Williams. I think he just made it up—never have found anyone who's ever heard of it.

Sometimes I drink whiskey, sometimes I drink wine
But I'll take a true brew, any old time.

Refrain: That friend of mine
has taken my liquor
from me.

Refrain:

# WILDWOOD FLOWER

That old favorite of the Carter Family.

50

# FLOP EARED MULE

Note in part A measure 5 where the thumb plays the 5th string on a downbeat, followed by a brush sequence. In part B the whole part can be done by barring with the index finger across the first three strings at the seventh fret, and using the 2nd and 3rd finger to reach the other notes.

# DOUBLE FILE

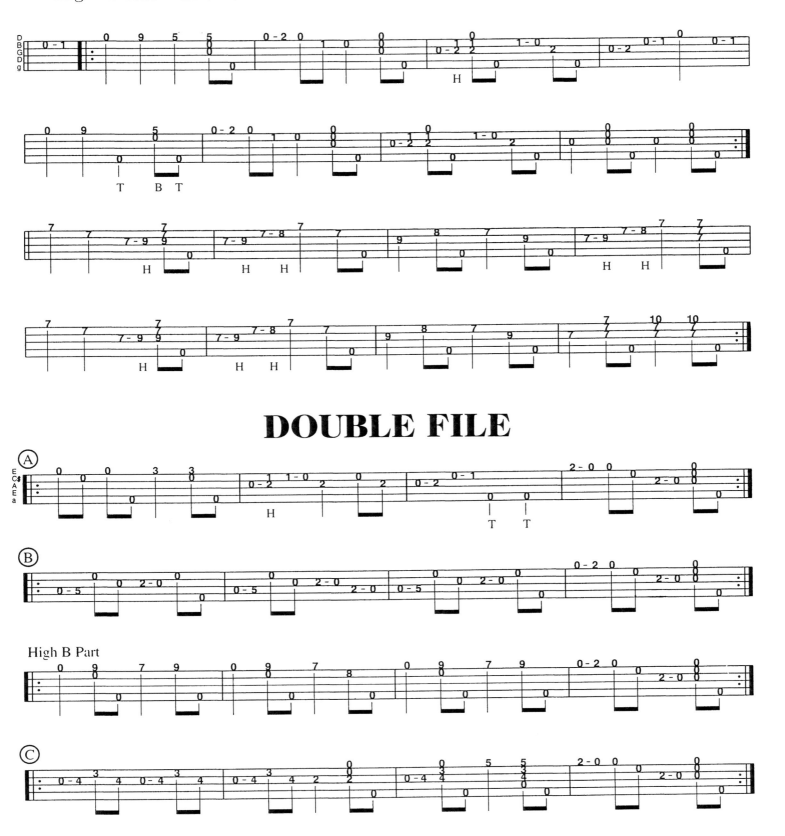

51

# LIZA JANE

A popular old tune. Be careful in part B, measure 6 where the brush sequence is played on the downbeat instead of the upbeat as is usual. Doing it this way gives an interesting focus to the rhythm of the piece; just don't lose the rhythm after doing it!

# SANTA CLAUS COME AND GONE

Thanks to the Northern Broadcasters of Eugene, Oregon, for this great old-time tune; sounds best on a fretless banjo. The roll in part A marked with an R below the tab is produced by striking down over the strings with the index and then thumbing the fifth string at the downbeat of the next measure. To see (hear) how this sounds without a roll, refer to the *.

part B is repeated from tunes

etc.

52

# GOT A LITTLE HOME TO GO TO

The timing here is set slightly off from the usual. In a few places the chord is brushed on the down beat instead of the up beat as is usual. Close attention to the tab for part A particularly is required to get the timing correct; the fingering is simple and straightforward.

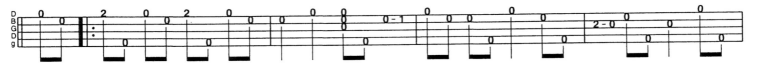

# CONCLUSION

These tunes represent the way I hear a fiddle tune and what I play on the banjo to complement and enrich that music. They are intended to give you ideas and are not to be regarded as the one and only way of rendering a tune. Take them, change them, turn them inside out and upside down. Put your own inspirations and spontaneity into them. The life of you and the music will be enriched by it.

Address any questions or comments to:

Alec Slater
c/o Mel Bay Publications
P.O. Box 66
Pacific, MO 63069

Alec Slater

# FOREWORD

The first time I saw Lisa, she was leading a horse much larger than both of us into a barn at Heartwood Farm in Hopkinton, Rhode Island. Little did I know then that this strong, sure woman and I would go on to form not just a close friendship, but one of the most satisfying musical relationships I have ever known.

At that time, I was not very familiar with either old-time music or the clawhammer style of banjo playing; however, I admired Lisa's clean, aggressive style, and her determination to expand it to Celtic and other styles of music. I play an instrument without a clear tradition in either American or Celtic music (English system concertina), and Lisa's unwillingness to be bound by "possibilities" and "limits" has been a constant inspiration in my own musical growth. If it can be done on five-string banjo, Lisa can do it.

May Terri

# INTRODUCTION

The following tablatures are arrangements for clawhammer banjo. This collection includes jigs, reels, polkas, hornpipes, strathspreys, waltzes and songs from Ireland, Scotland, the Shetland Islands, Cape Breton, New England and Southern Appalachia.

# ACKNOWLEDGMENTS

Special thanks to Steve Morse and Kevin Desabrais for their guitar accompaniment; Frank Palaia, Monkey Sound Studio, May Terri, Jack Wright, Dave Pugh, Ken Sweeney, Aubrey Atwater, Elwood Donnelly and Elizabeth Morse, with whom I've had the pleasure of playing these tunes; and my family, Paul, Mike, Matty, Mom and Dad, for their continued support.

Lisa F. Schmitz

# ROLLING WAVES
## (Irish Jig)

# PADDY'S RETURN
## (Irish Double Jig)

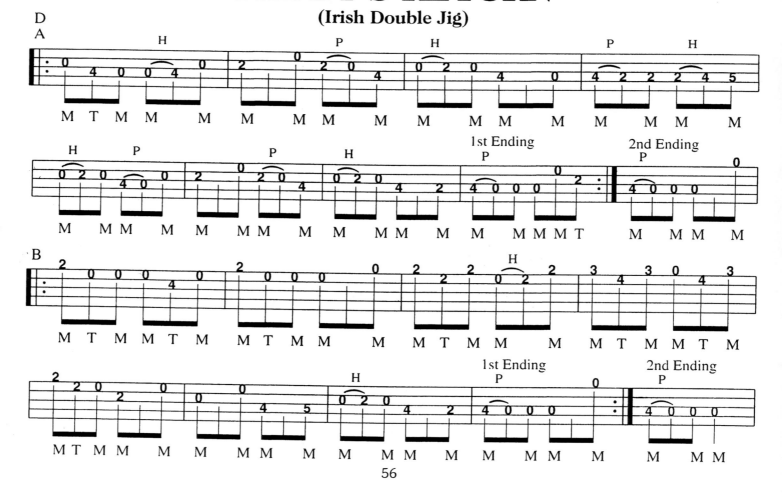

# THE BURNT OLD MAN

## (Irish Jig)

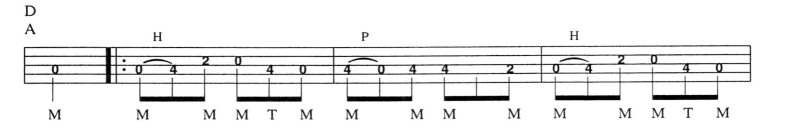

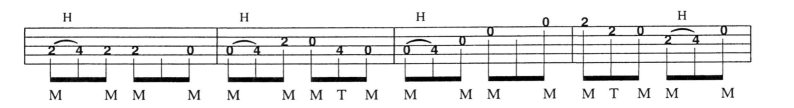

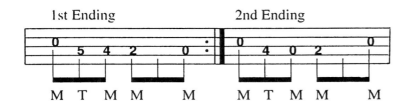

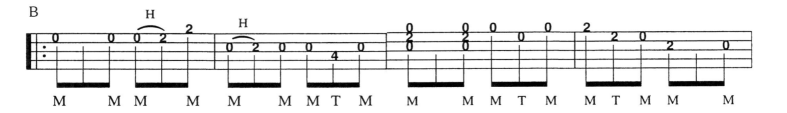

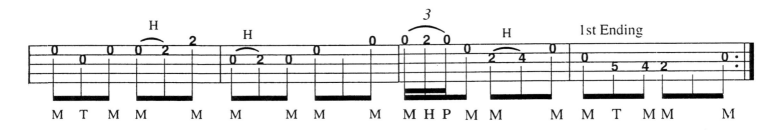

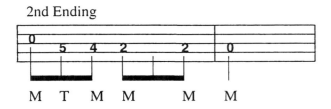

# THE BLARNEY PILGRIM
## (Irish Jig)

* NOTE: traditionally played in D, capo 7th fret

# THE RAKES OF KILDARE

## (Irish Double Jig)

Amodal

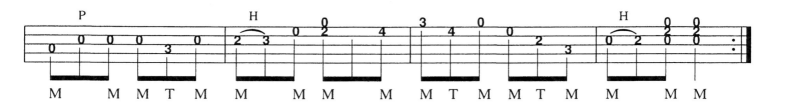

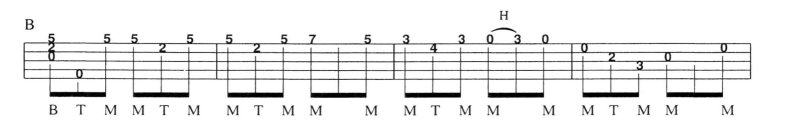

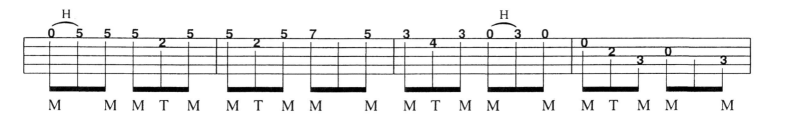

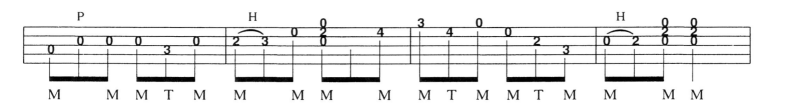

# CLIFFS OF MOHER
## (Irish Jig)

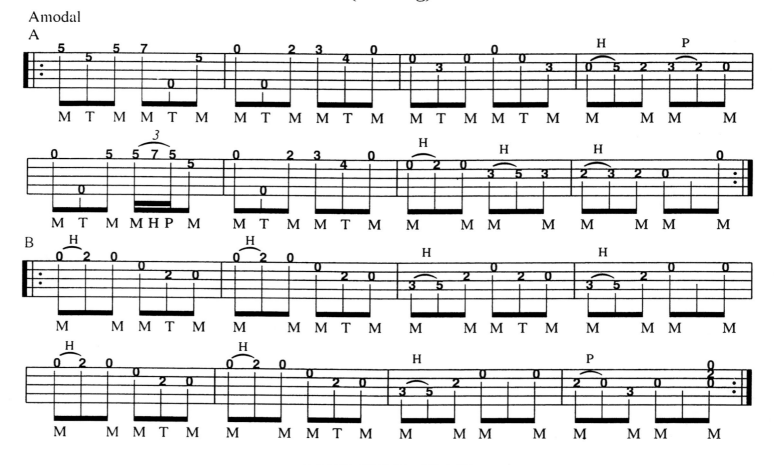

# KESH JIG
## (Irish Jig)

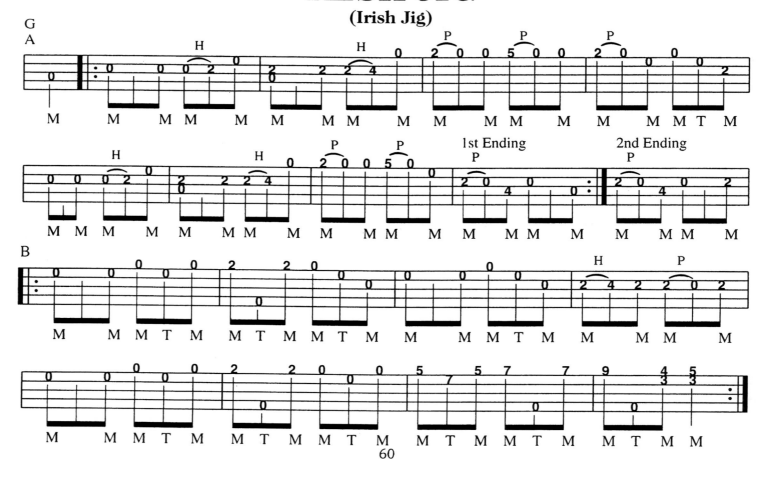

# SWAGGERING JIG

## (Irish Slip-Jig)

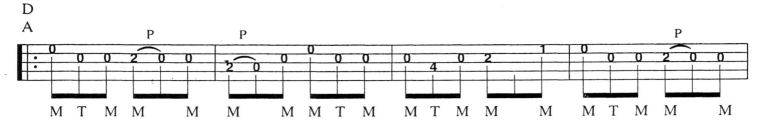

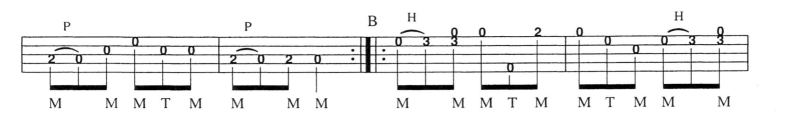

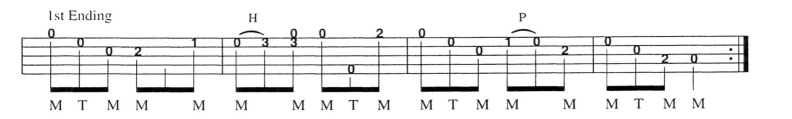

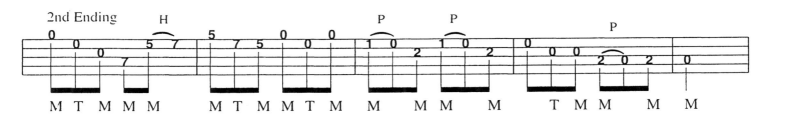

# SOUTHWIND
## (Irish Waltz)

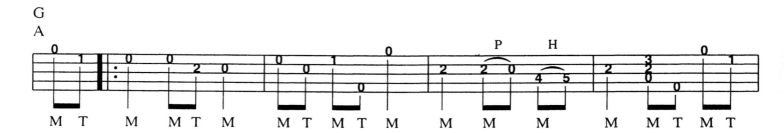

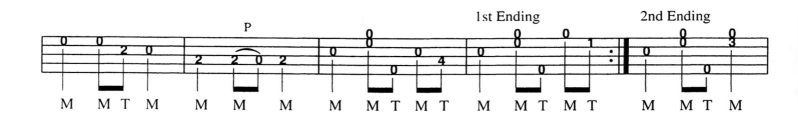

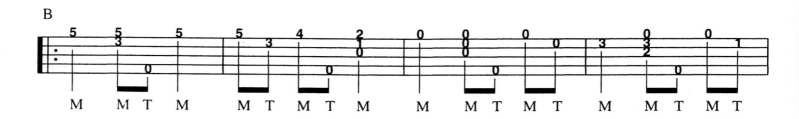

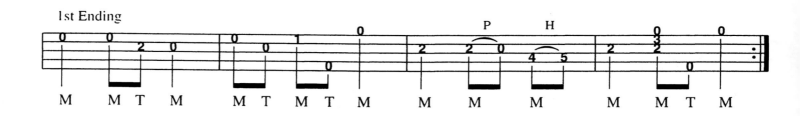

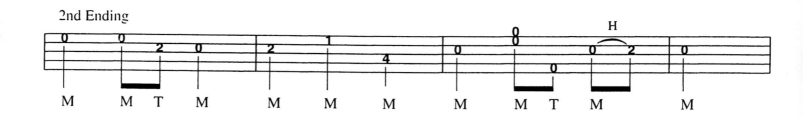

# WHERE THE AUBEG FLOWS

**(Irish Waltz)**

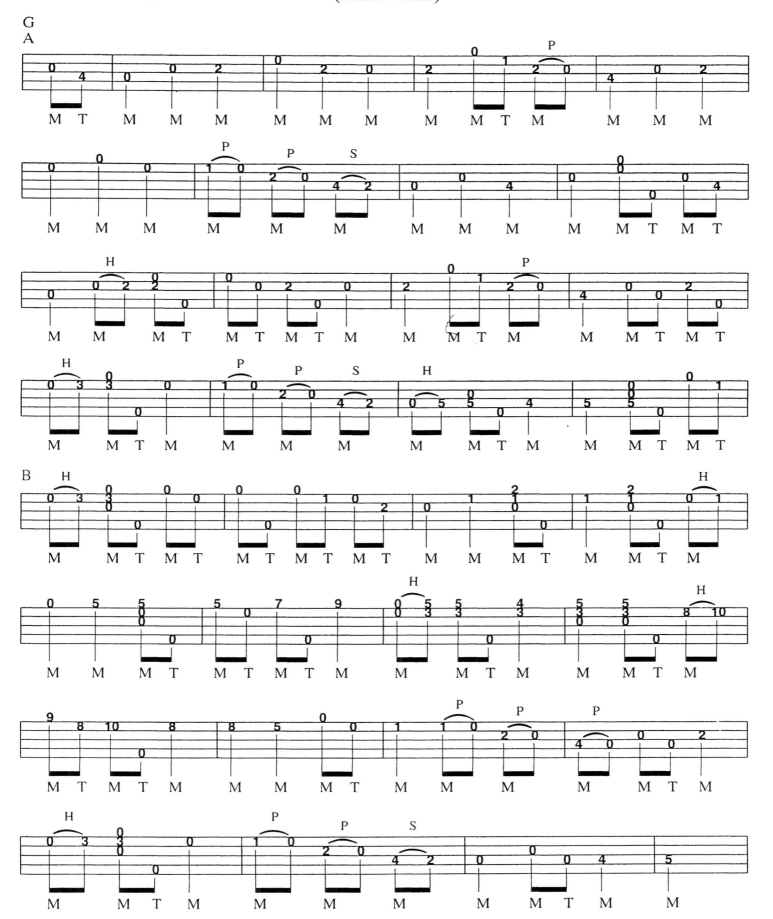

# TEMPERANCE REEL

## (Irish Reel)

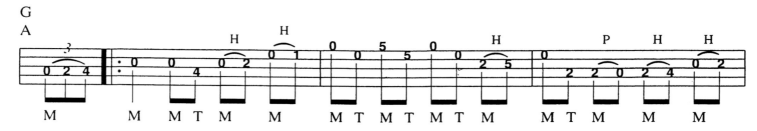

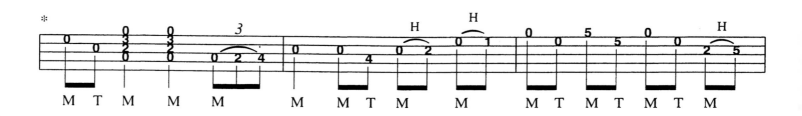

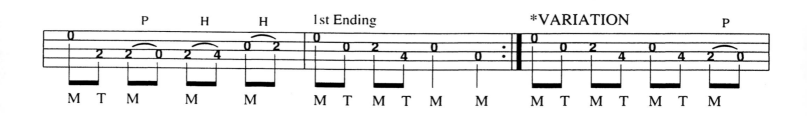

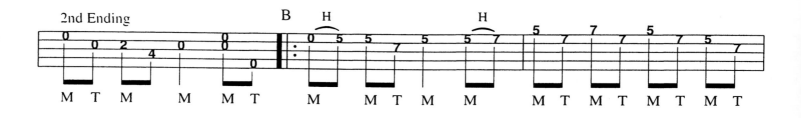

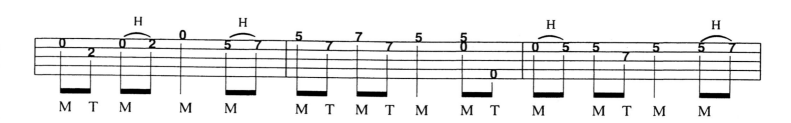

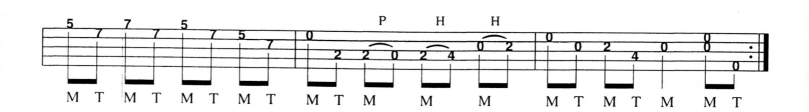

# CREEL OF TURF

## (Jig)

Amodal *

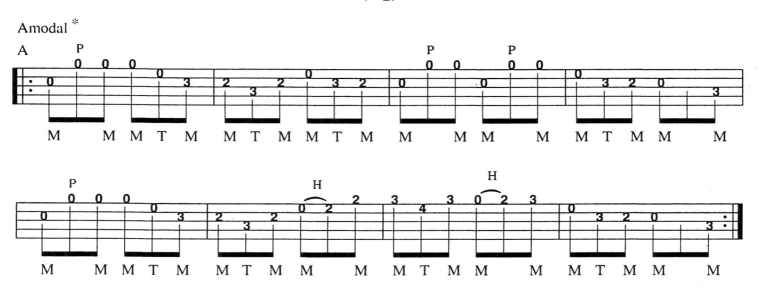

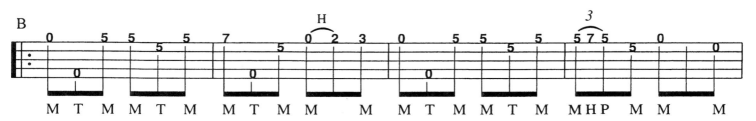

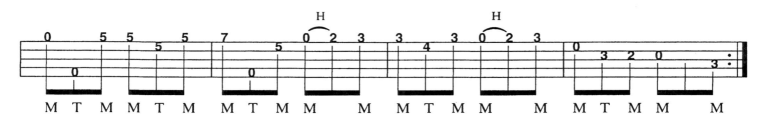

*Traditionally played in Em (Capo 7).

Final Ending

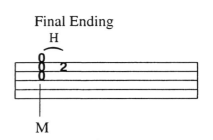

# PLANXTY MADAME MAXWELL

## (Irish, O'Carolan)

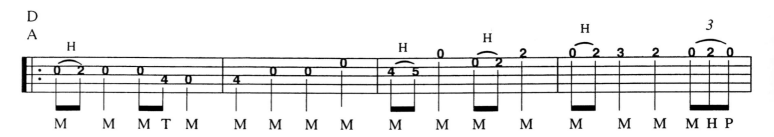

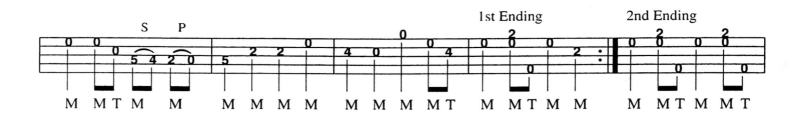

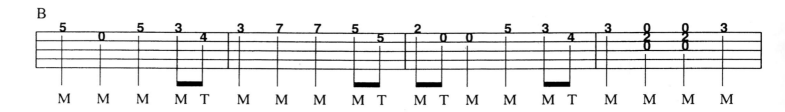

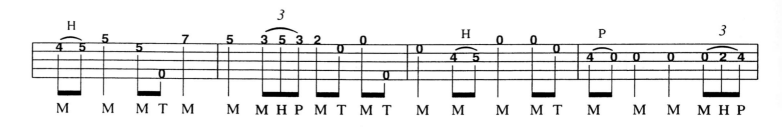

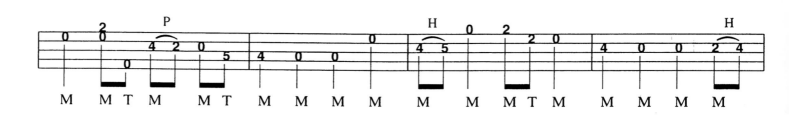

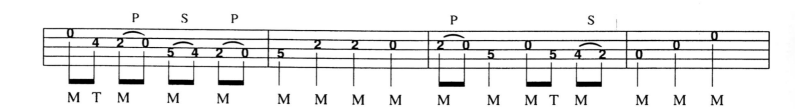

# FRIEZE BREETCHES

## (Irish Double Jig)

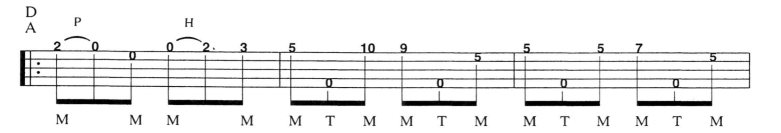

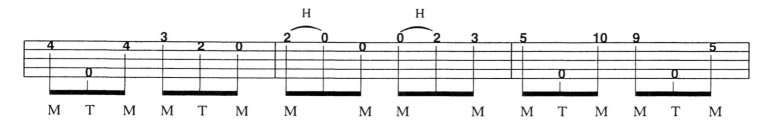

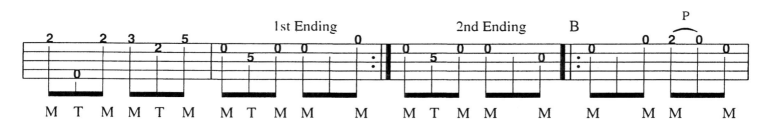

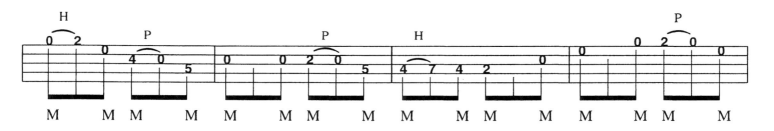

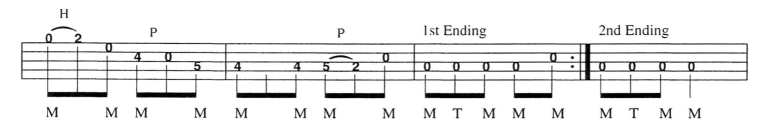

C

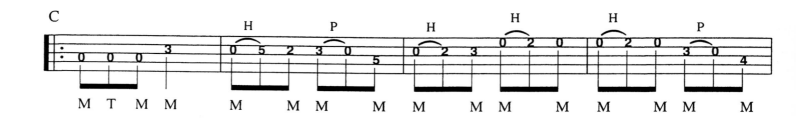

D

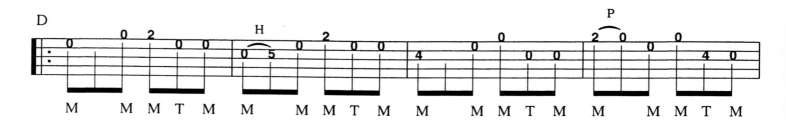

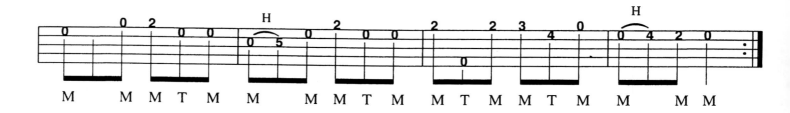

E

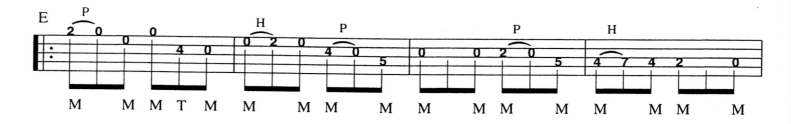

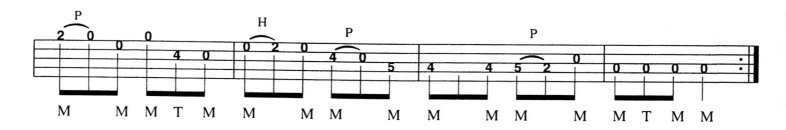

# COME DANCE AND SING

### (New England Reel)

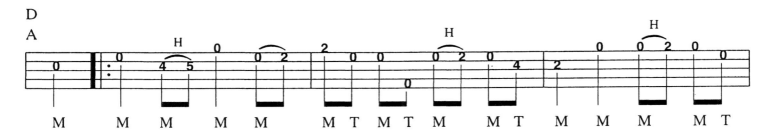

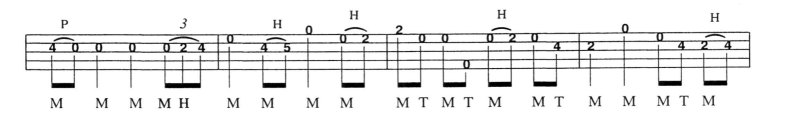

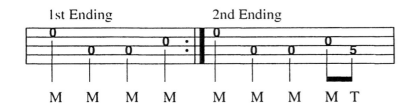

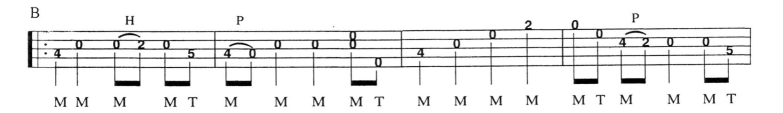

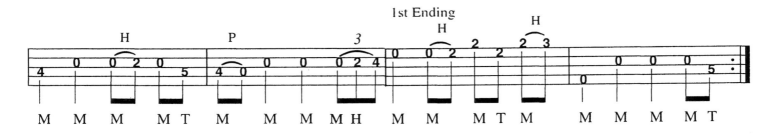

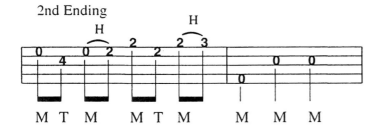

# THE ATHOLL HIGHLANDERS I
## (Scottish March)

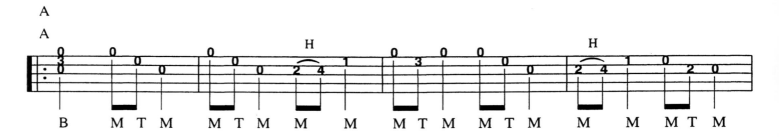

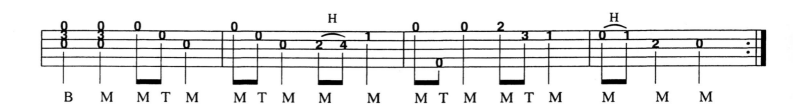

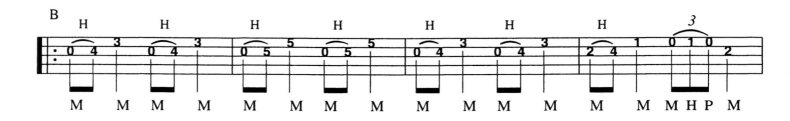

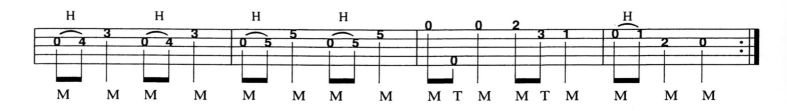

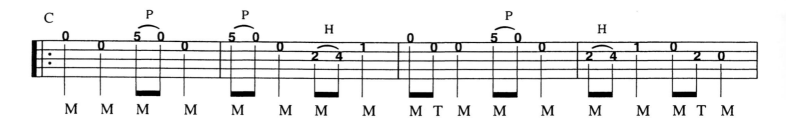

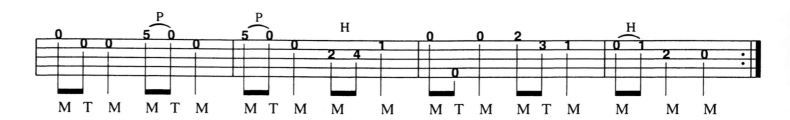

# THE ATHOLL HIGHLANDERS II
### (Scottish March)

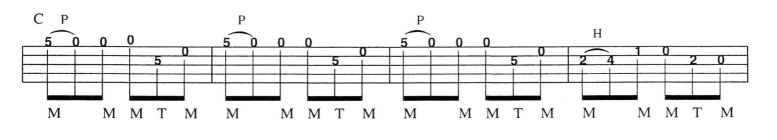

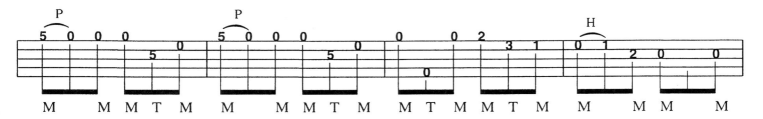

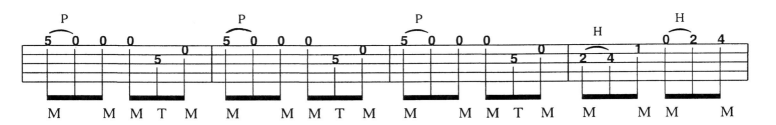

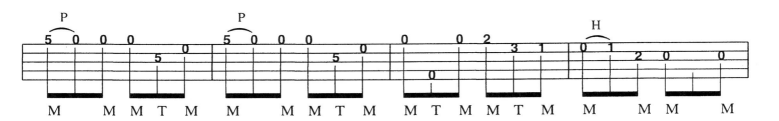

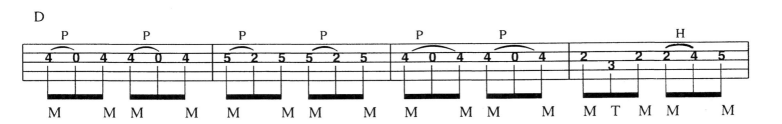

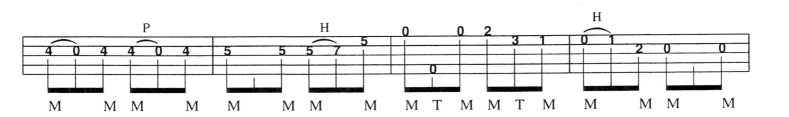

# OUT ON THE OCEAN

**(Irish Jig)**

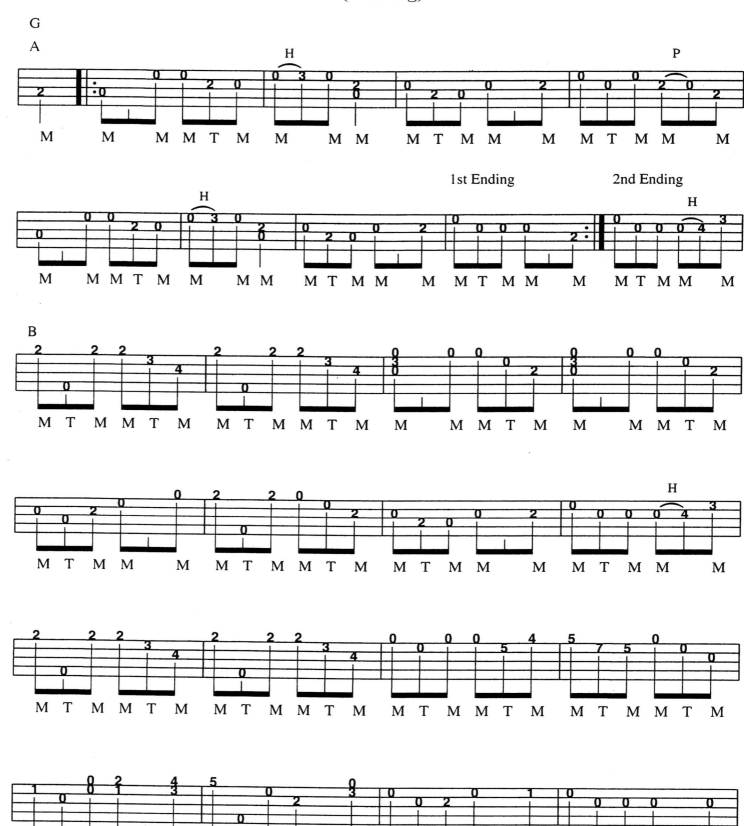

# TOM BILLEY'S JIG

## (Irish Jig)

Amodal

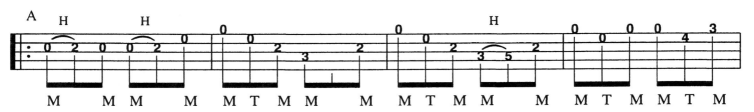

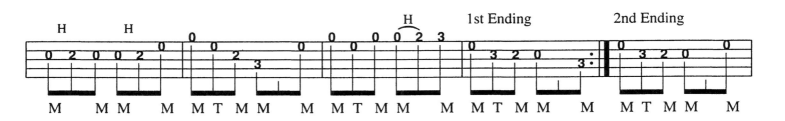

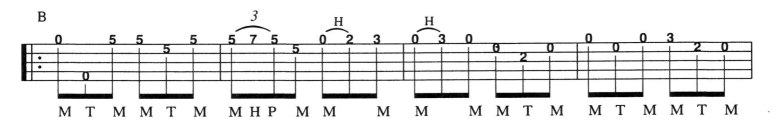

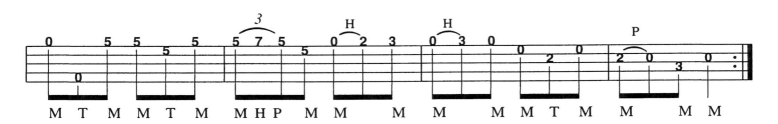

# PRINCE WILLIAM
## (New England)

# PRINCE WILLIAM
## (Variation)

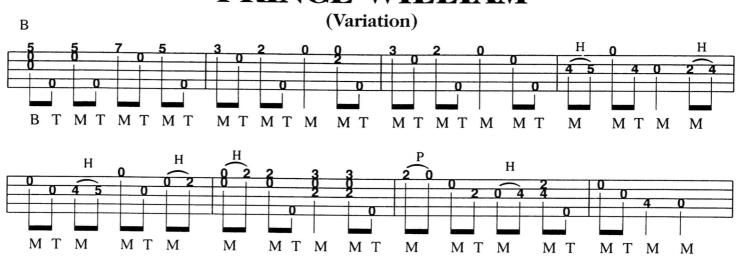

# KNOLE PARK
## (English Country Dance)

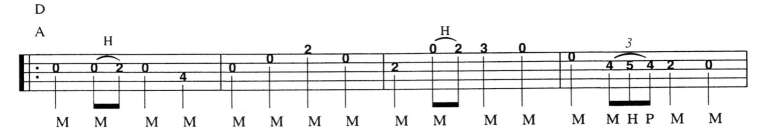

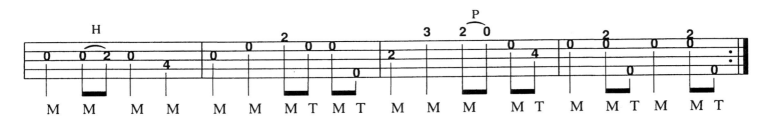

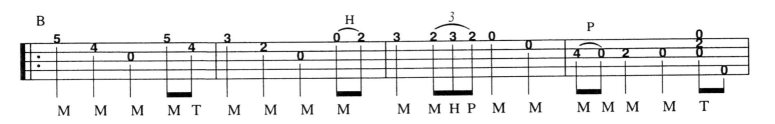

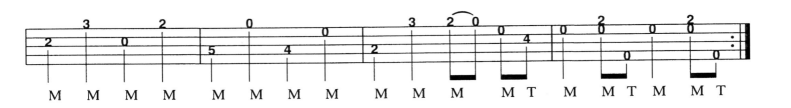

# RED WING
## (American)

# PETRONELLA
## (New England)

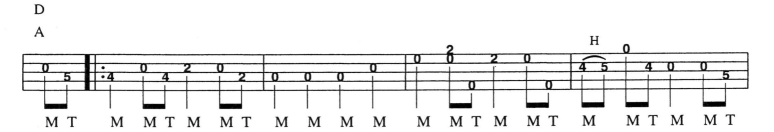

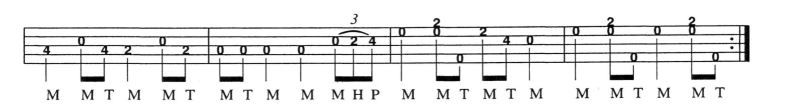

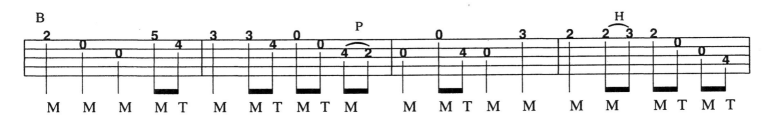

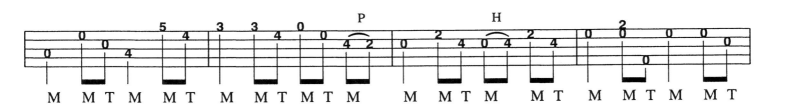

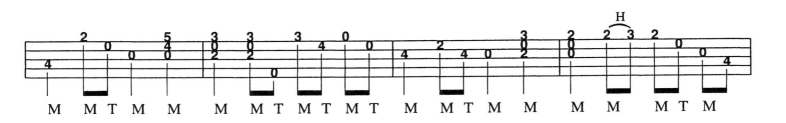

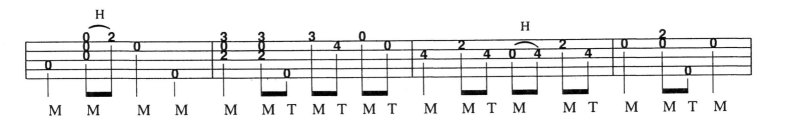

# PRETTY PEG
### (Irish)

# COLORED ARISTOCRACY
### (Old-Time)

# LADY OF THE LAKE

(New England)

# NANCY
### (Shetland March)

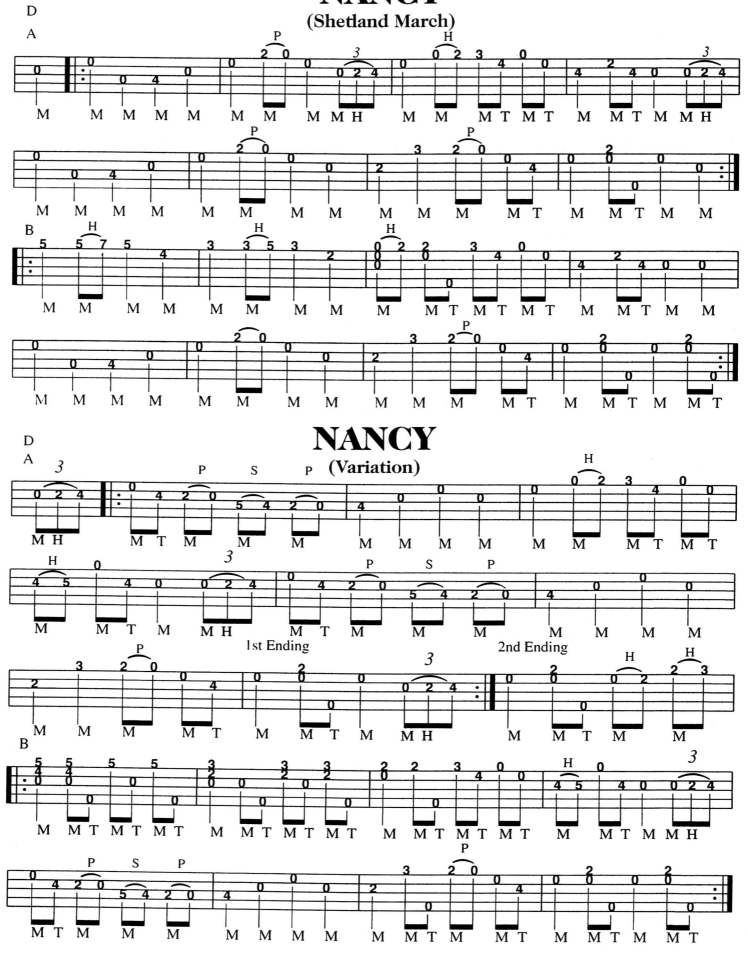

# NANCY
### (Variation)

# DENNIS MURPHY'S POLKA
## (Irish Polka)

# 42-POUND CHECK
## (Irish Polka)

# JOHN RYAN'S POLKA
## (Irish Polka)

# JIMMY ALLEN
## (English Country Dance)

# SCOTSMAN OVER THE BORDER

## (Scottish Jig)

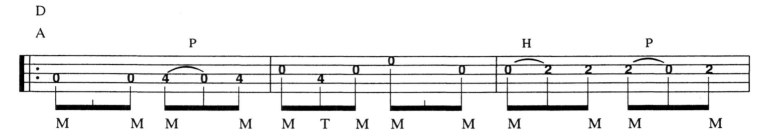

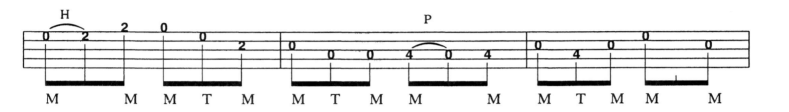

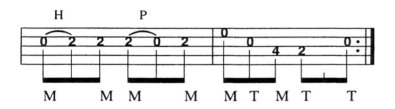

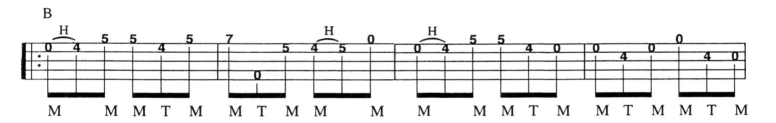

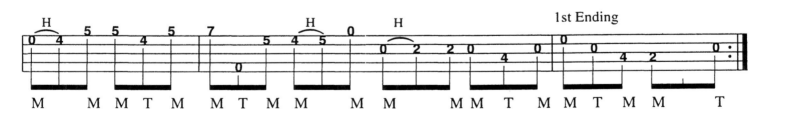

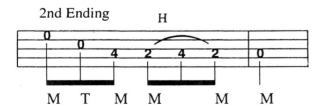

# PADDY CLANCY'S

## (Irish Jig)

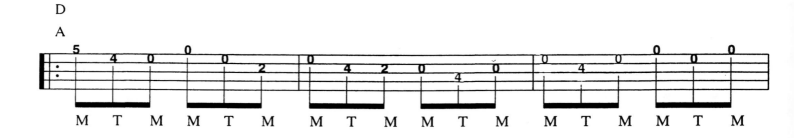

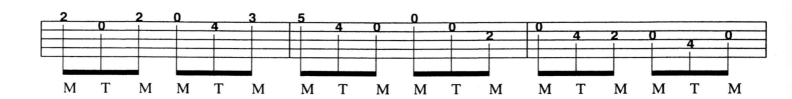

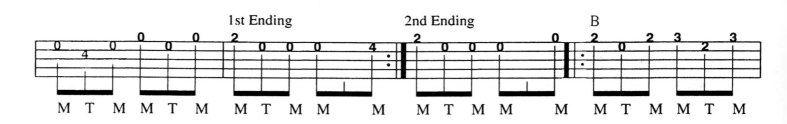

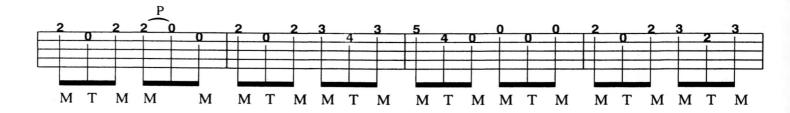

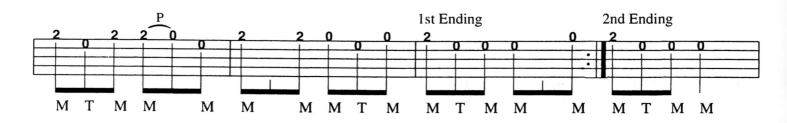

# ICE ON THE POND
## (New England)

*G Tuning

# PATSY GEARY'S
## (Irish Jig)

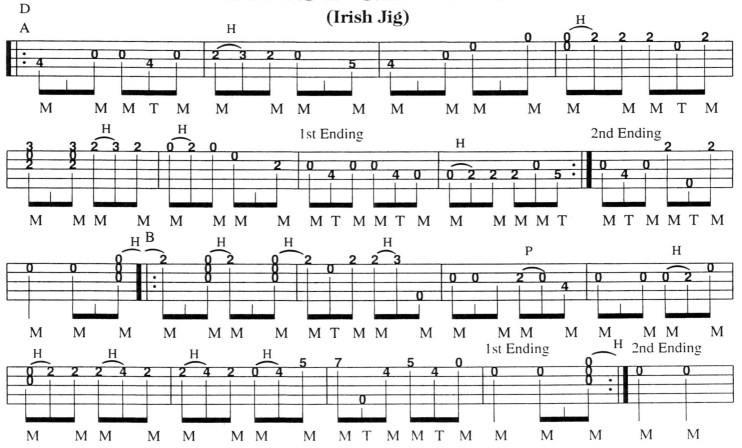

# SWANEE RIVER

## (American)

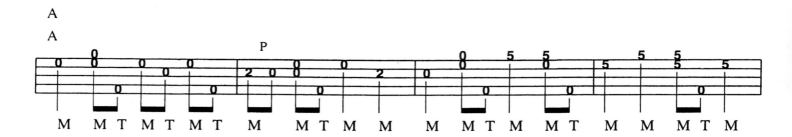

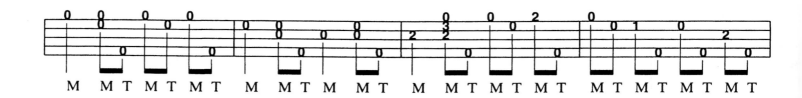

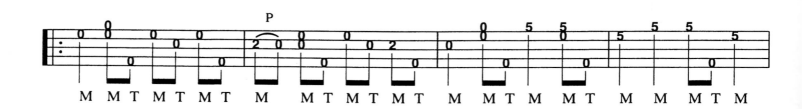

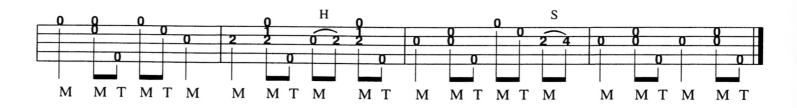

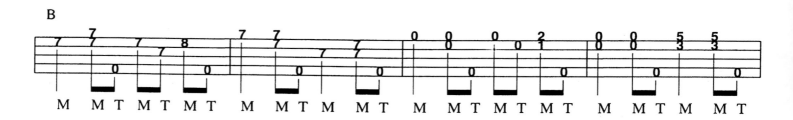

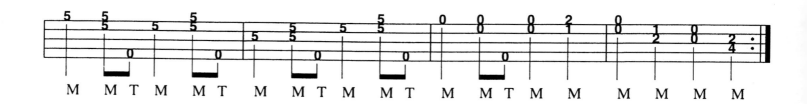

# BLACKBERRY BLOSSOM

## (Old-Time)

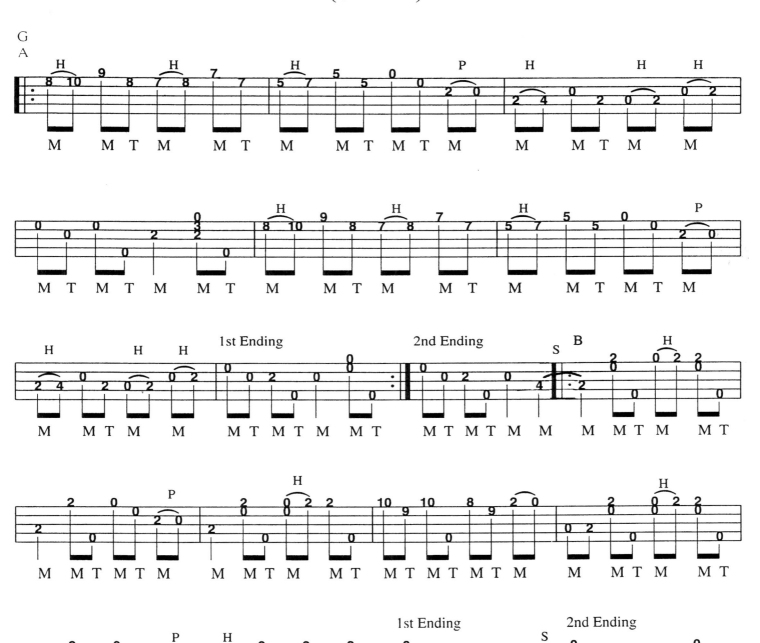

# MISS GORDON OF PARK

## (Scottish Jig)

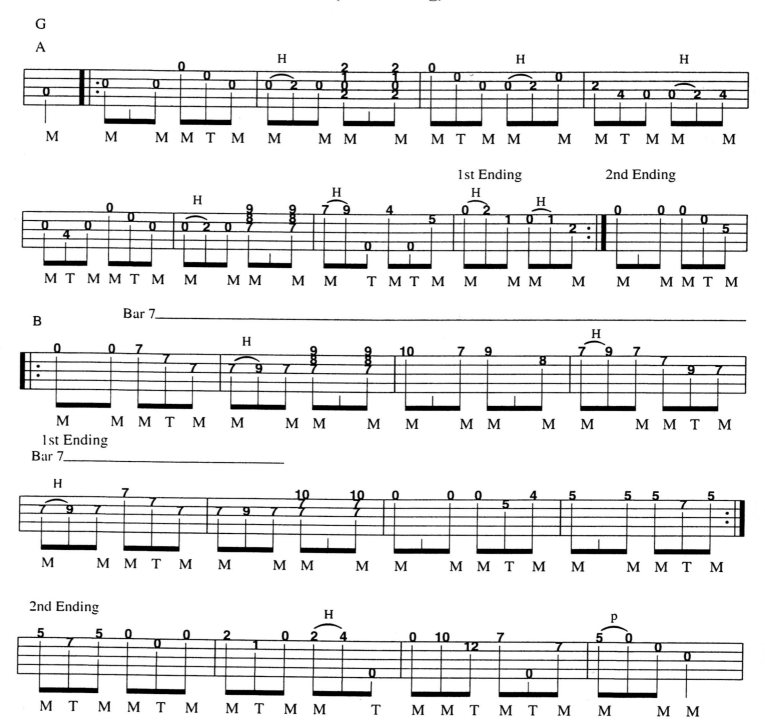

# TAR ROAD TO SLIGO

## (Irish Jig)

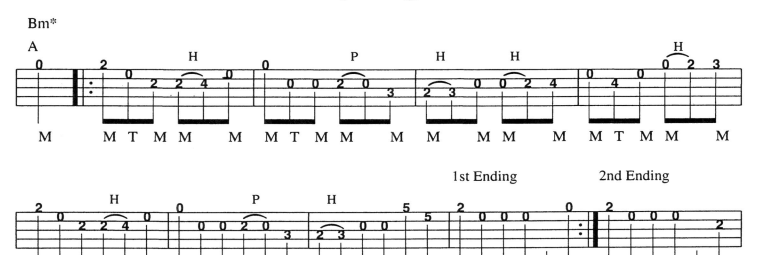

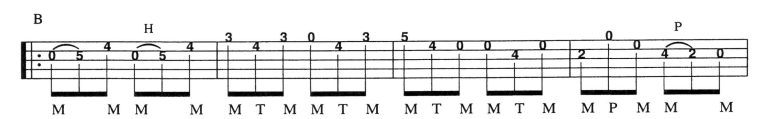

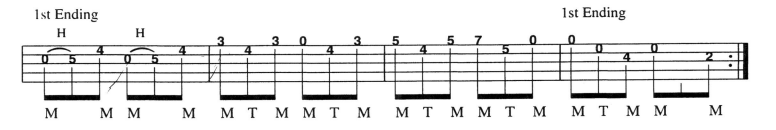

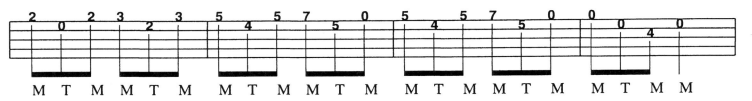

\* Amodal tuning

# COLEMAN'S CROSS

## (Irish Jig)

Bm*

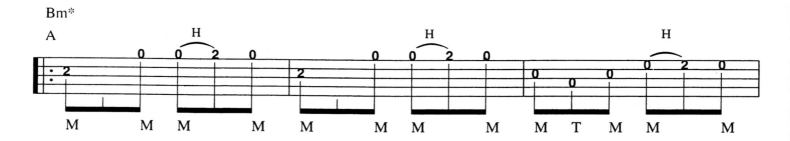

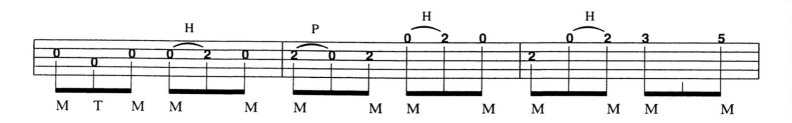

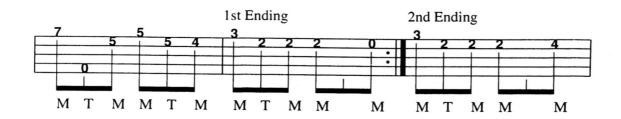

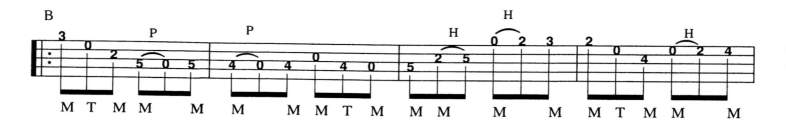

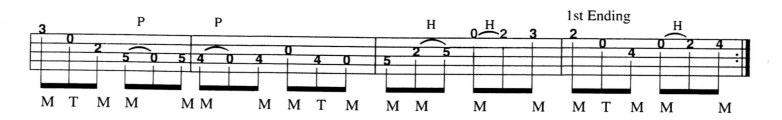

2nd Ending

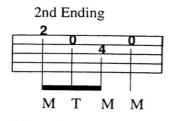

* D tuning

# MAGGIE BROWN'S FAVORITE

### (Irish Single Jig)

# MISS WEDDERBURN'S REEL

## (Scottish Reel)

E (Double C / Capo 4)

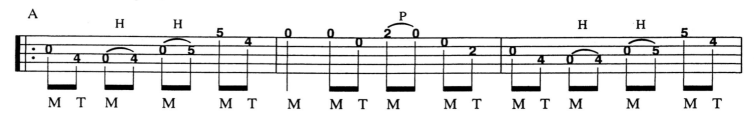

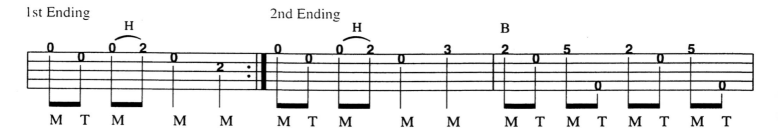

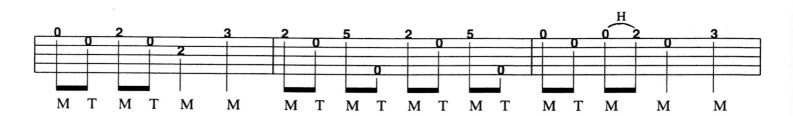

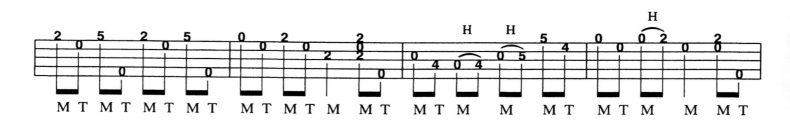

# DR. O'NEIL'S
### (Irish Jig)

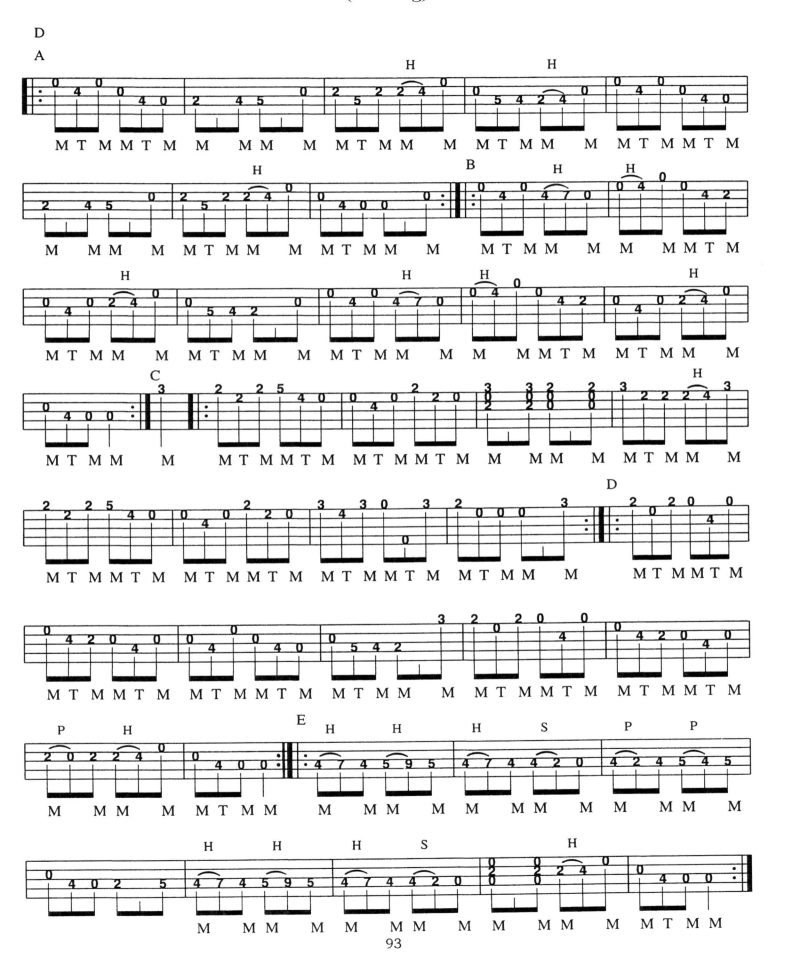

# PIPE ON THE HOB

## (Irish Double Jig)

# THE MUNSTER BUTTERMILK

### (Irish Single Jig)

# GREEN MOUNTAIN PETRONELLA

## (New England)

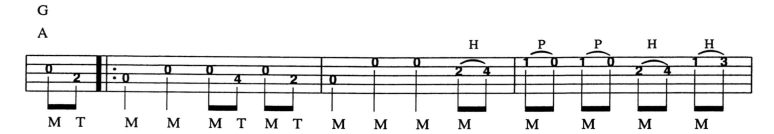

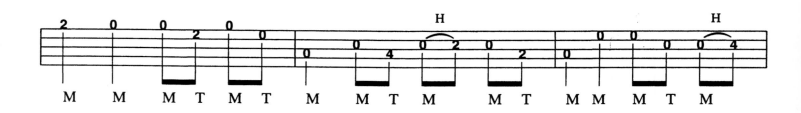

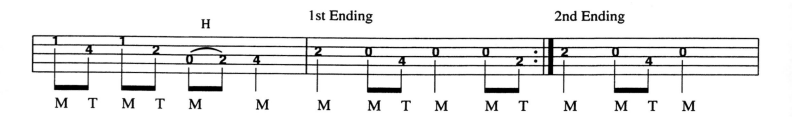

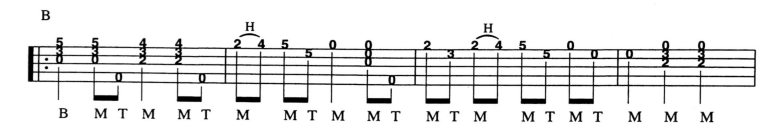

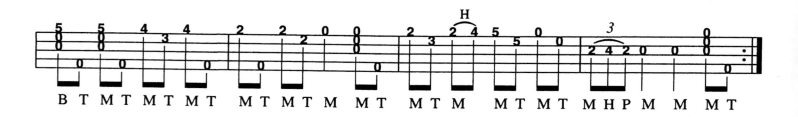

# FAREWELL TO WHISKY

## (Irish Reel)

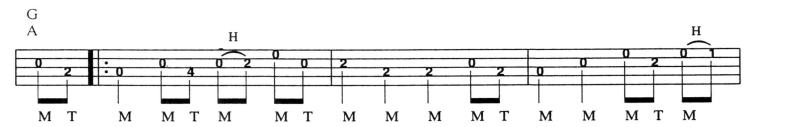

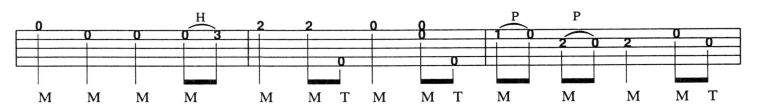

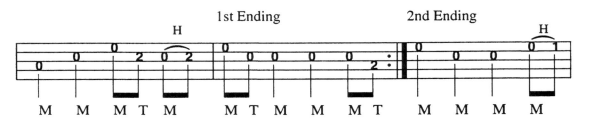

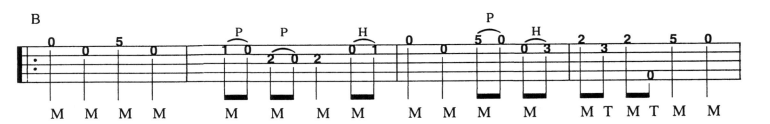

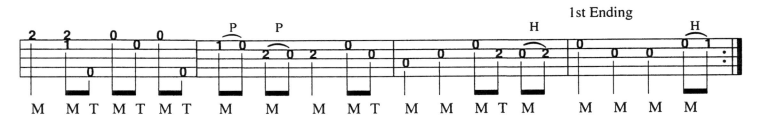

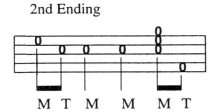

# HEATHER ON THE MOOR

## (Scottish)

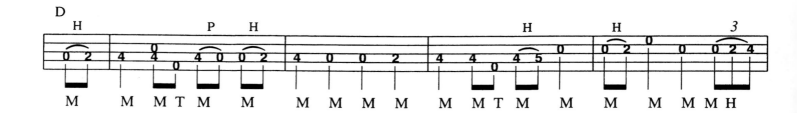

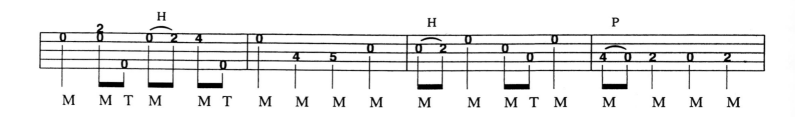

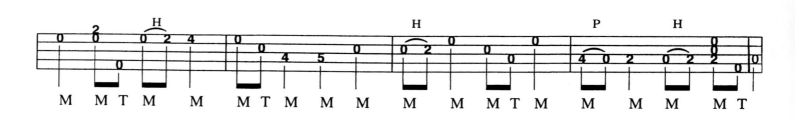

# SHEEBAG SHEEMORE
### (Irish)

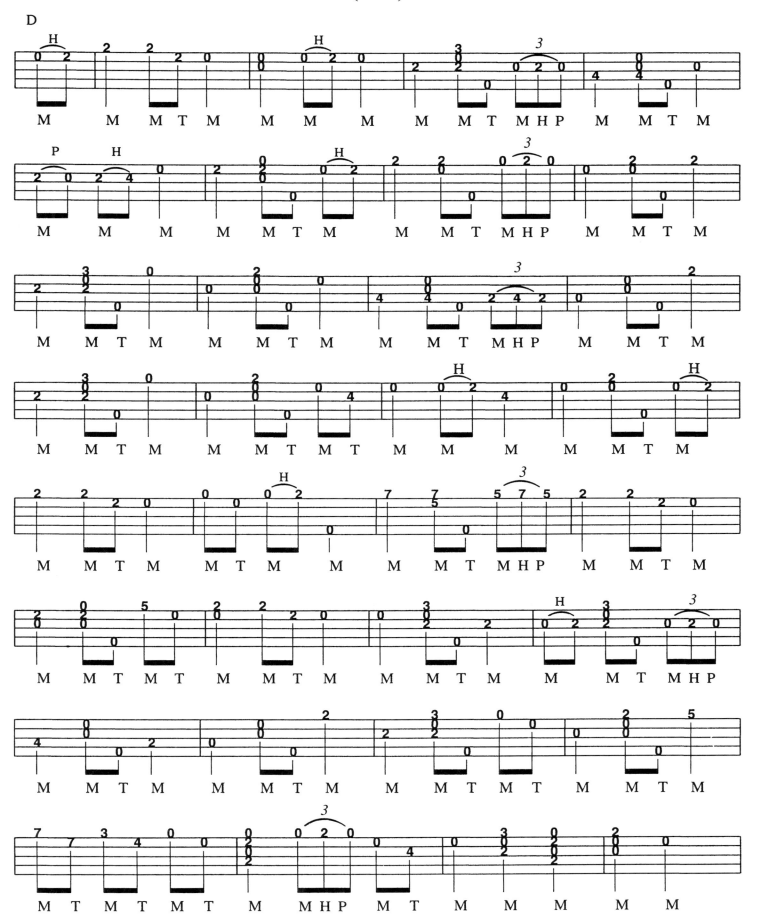

# CHRISTMAS DAY IDA MOARNIN'
## (Shetland)

# WASSAIL, WAISSAIL
## (English)

# NOEL, MERRILY ON HIGH

## (English)

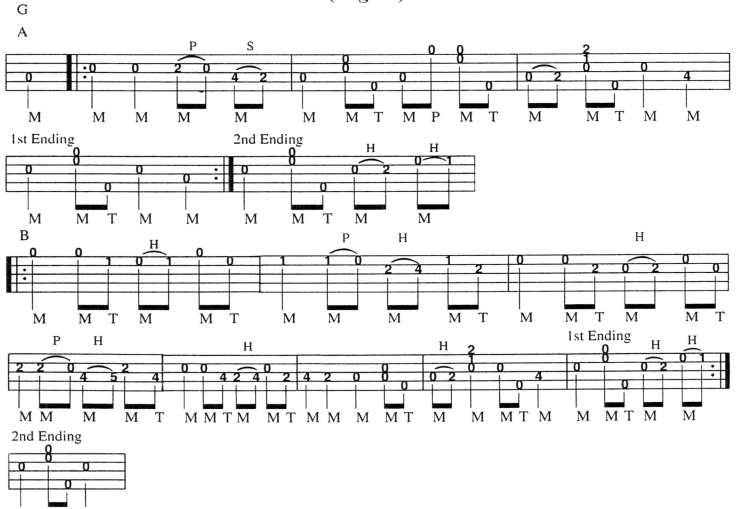

# OFF SHE GOES
## (British Isles Single Jig)

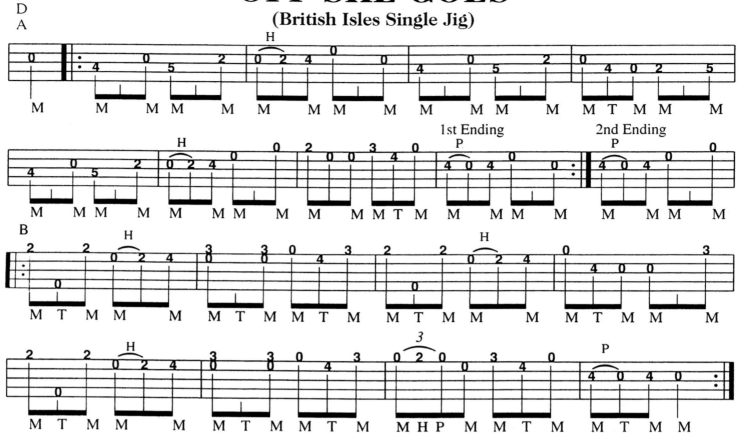

# HULL'S VICTORY
## (New England Hornpipe)

# OVER THE WATERFALL

## (Old-Time)

# GOLDEN SLIPPERS
## (Old-Time Reel)

# GIVE THE FIDDLER A DRAM
## (Old-Time)

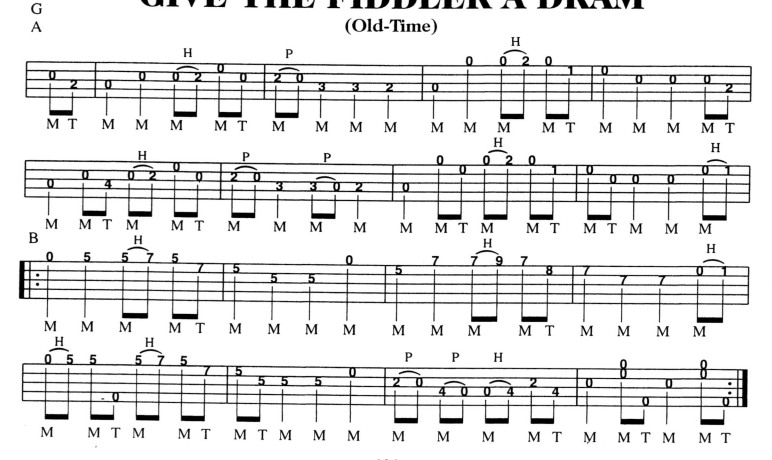

# RED RIVER VALLEY
### (American)

# TOUCH STONE
### (English Country Dance)

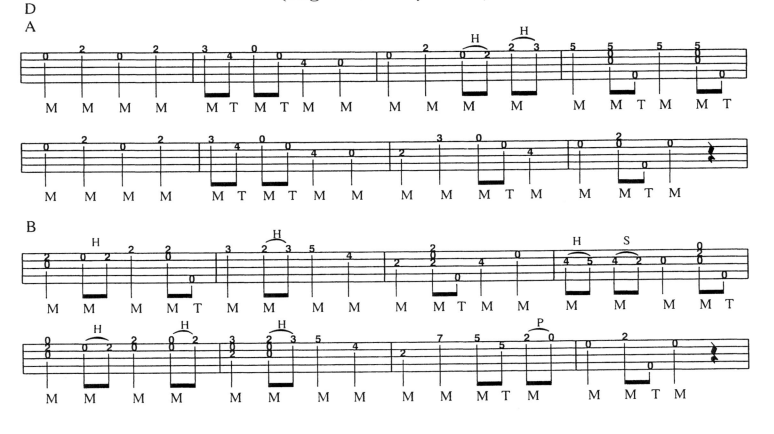

# RETURN FROM FINGAL
## (Irish)

Amodal

A

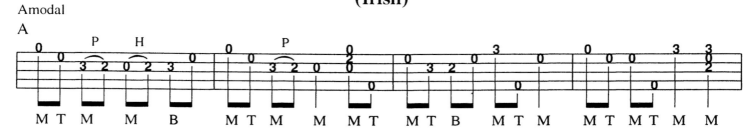

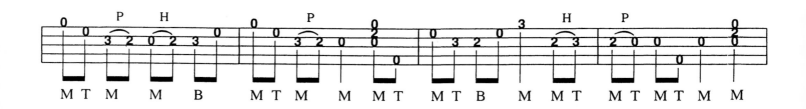

B

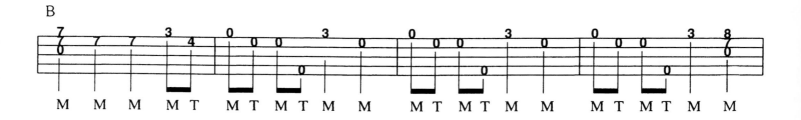

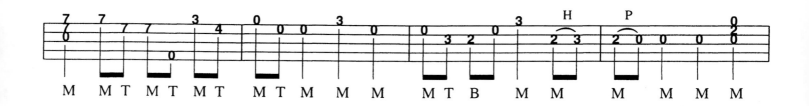

# THE MAID BEHIND THE BAR

### (Irish Reel)

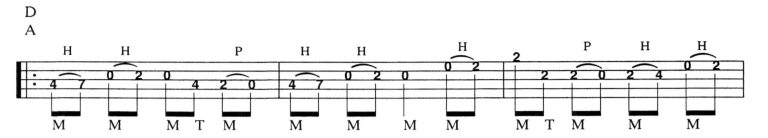

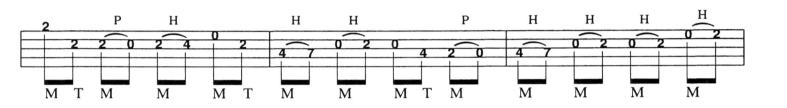

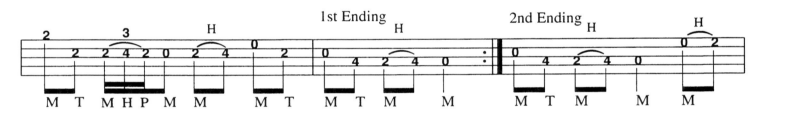

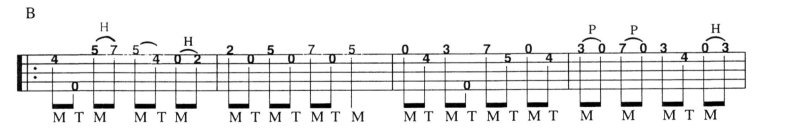

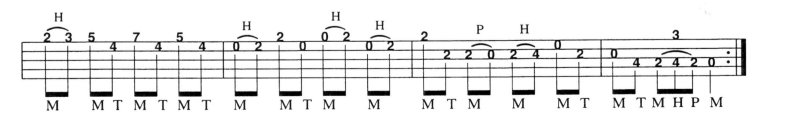

# THE ASHGROVE

## (English)

D
A

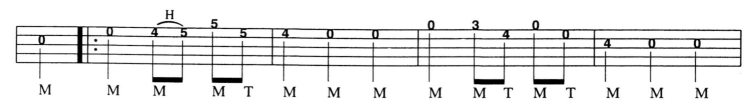

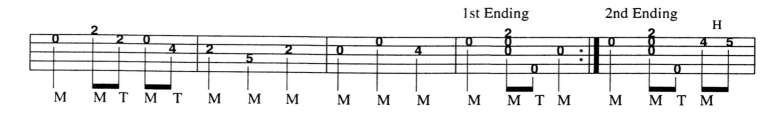

B

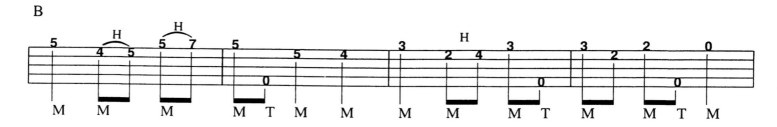

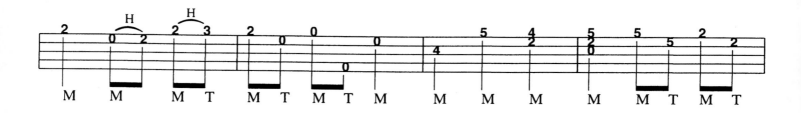

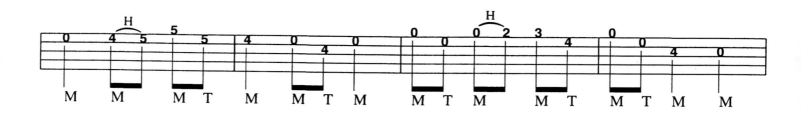

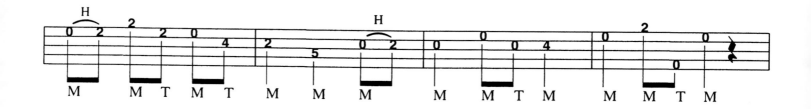

# THE HEWLETT

## (Irish, O'Carolan)

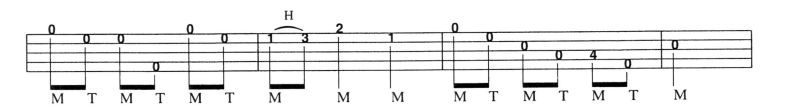

# MAY TERRI'S POLKA I
### (American/English)

# MAY TERRI'S POLKA II
### (American/English)

# LOUIE'S FIRST TUNE
## (New England Polka)

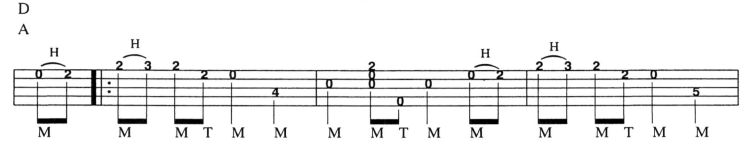

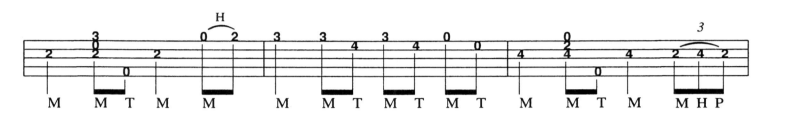

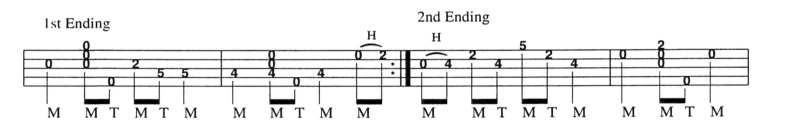

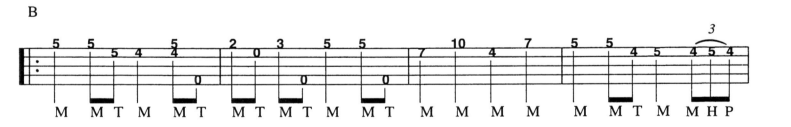

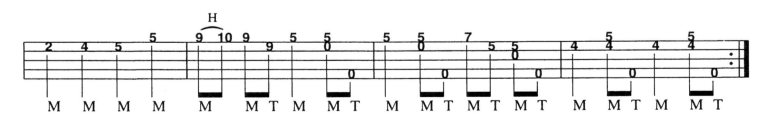

*Traditionally played in G.

# JESSICA'S POLKA
## (Irish Polka)

# THE GIRL I LEFT BEHIND ME
## (American)

# RED HAIRED BOY
## (Irish Reel)

# THE WHITE COCKADE
## (British Isles Reel)

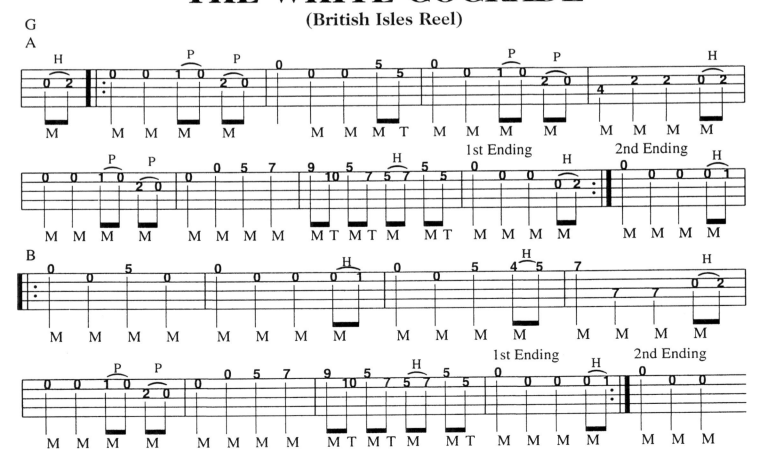

113

# PLANXTY GEORGE BRABAZON

## (Irish, O'Carolan)

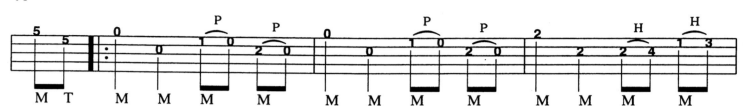

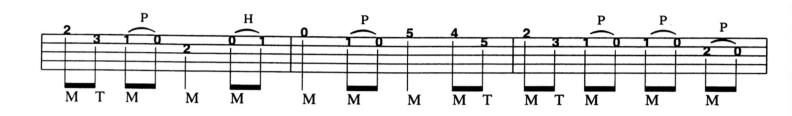

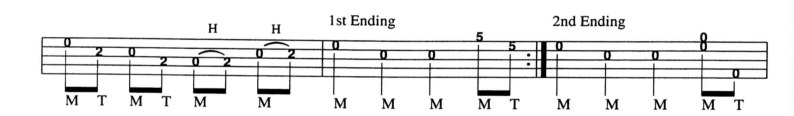

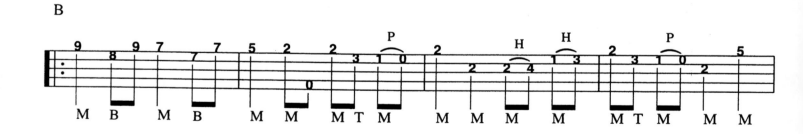

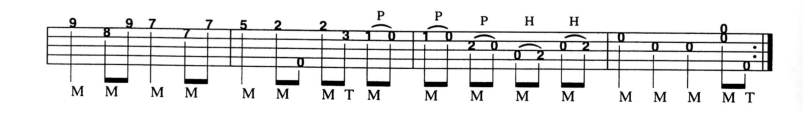

114

# ALABAMA JUBILEE

### (American)

G

# SONNY'S MAZURKA

## (Irish)

# MORGAN MAGAN

### (Irish, O'Carolan)

D*

Traditionally in G

# LORD INCHIQUIN

## (Irish, O'Carolan)

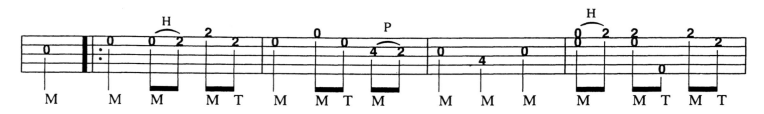

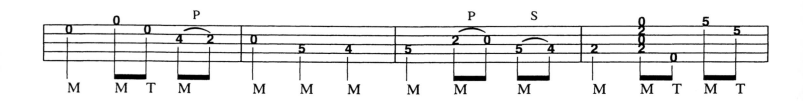

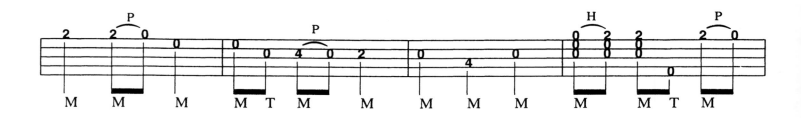

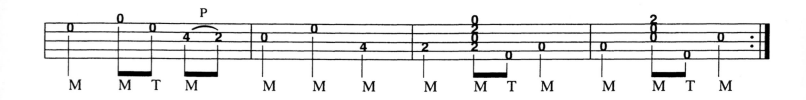

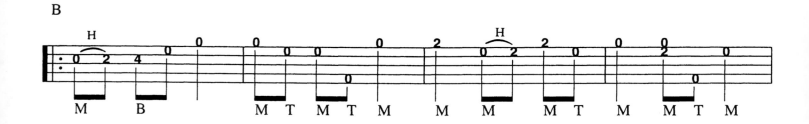

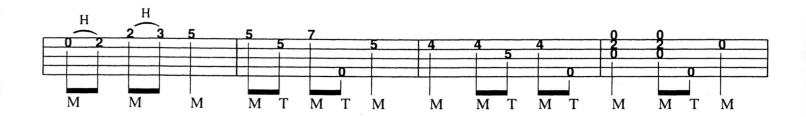

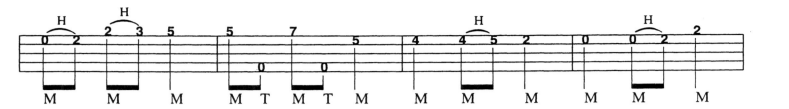

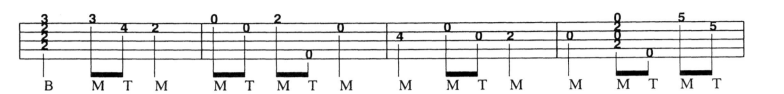

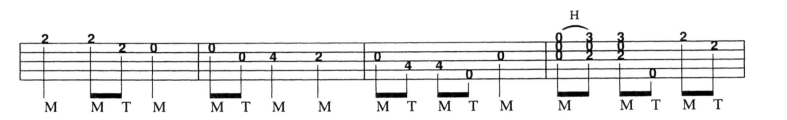

1st Ending      2nd Ending

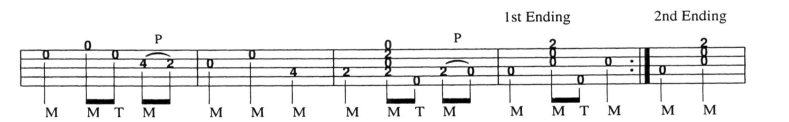

# COLD BLOW AND THE RAINY NIGHT

## (Irish)

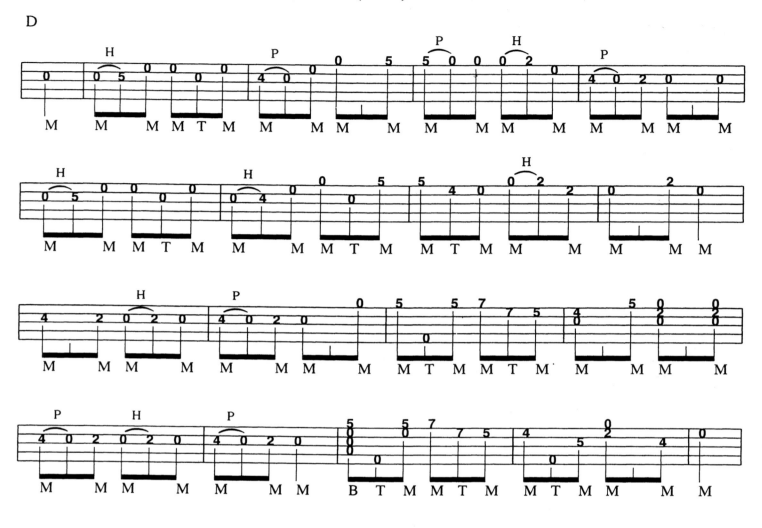

# FAIRY DANCE

## (Irish Reel)

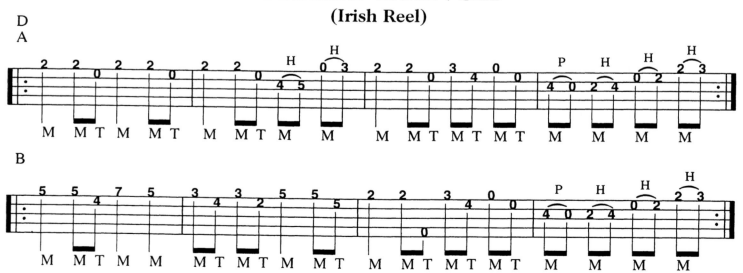

# THE BRAES OF MAR
## (Scottish Strathspey)

D
A

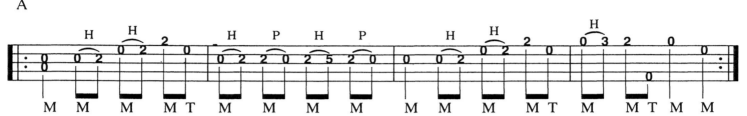

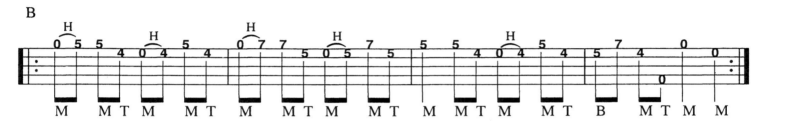

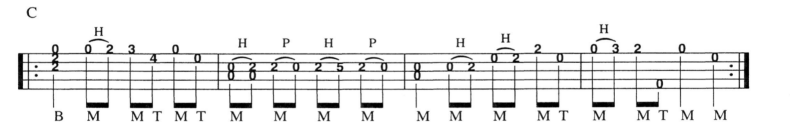

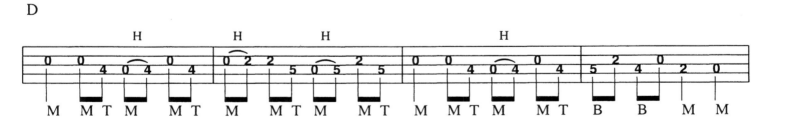

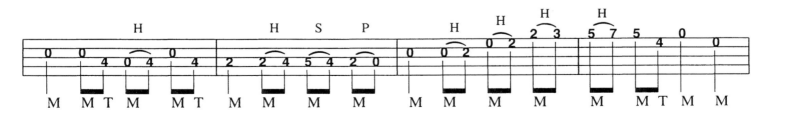

# EBENEZER
## (Old-Time)

# DONALD BLUE
## (Cape Breton)

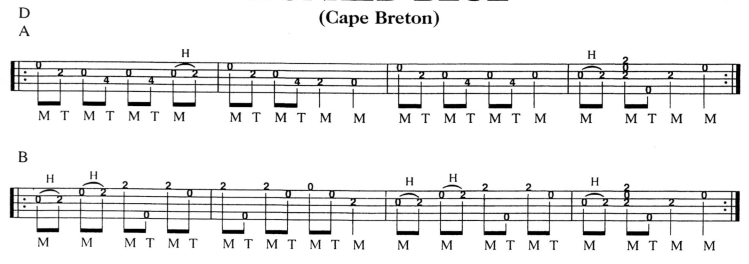

# SLEEP SOUNDA IDA MOURIN'

## (Shetland)

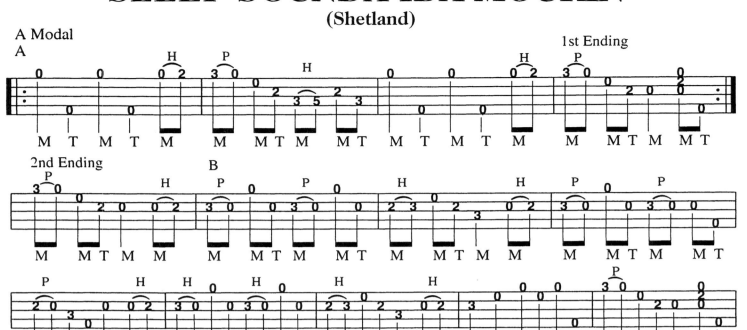

# MARKET TOWN

# RIDE A MILE

### (Irish Slip Jig)

G
A

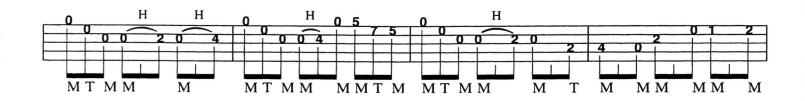

B

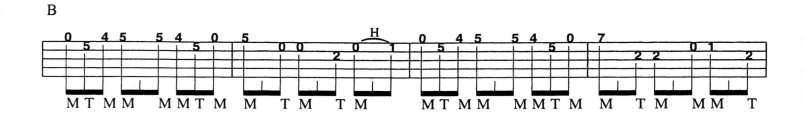

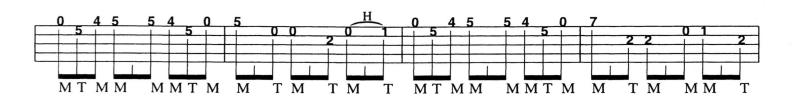

C

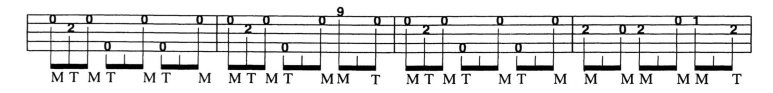

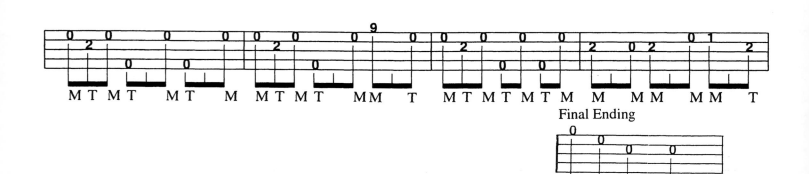

# JOHNNY TODD
### (Scottish)

# A POLKA
### (Irish Polka)

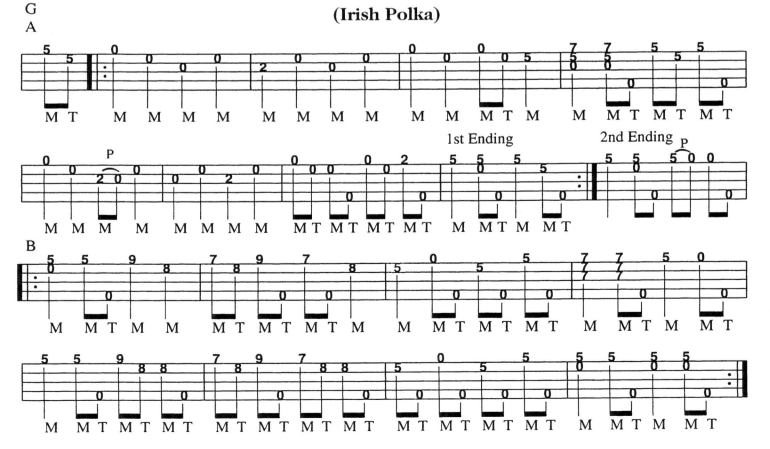

# JACK BROKE DA PRISON DOOR
## (Shetland)

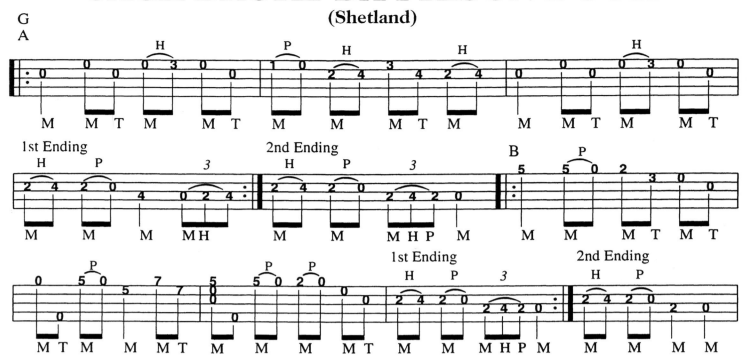

# ST. KILDA WEDDING
## (Scottish)

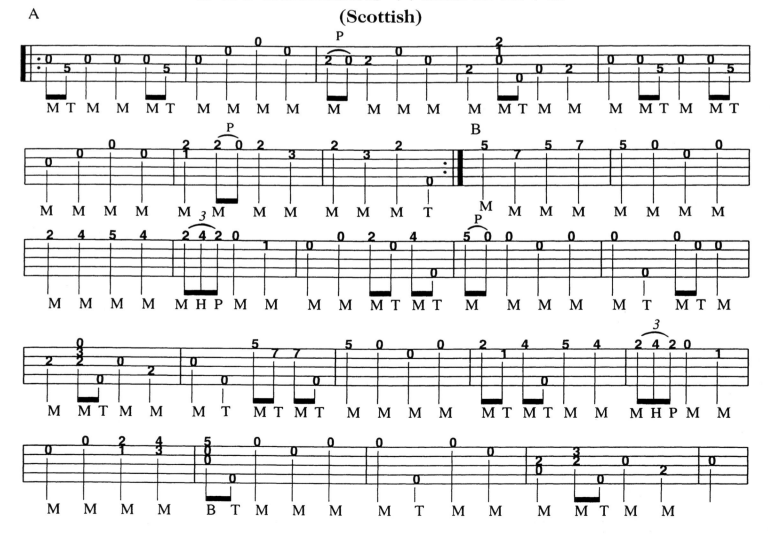

126

# PADDY ON THE RAILROAD
## (Irish Reel)

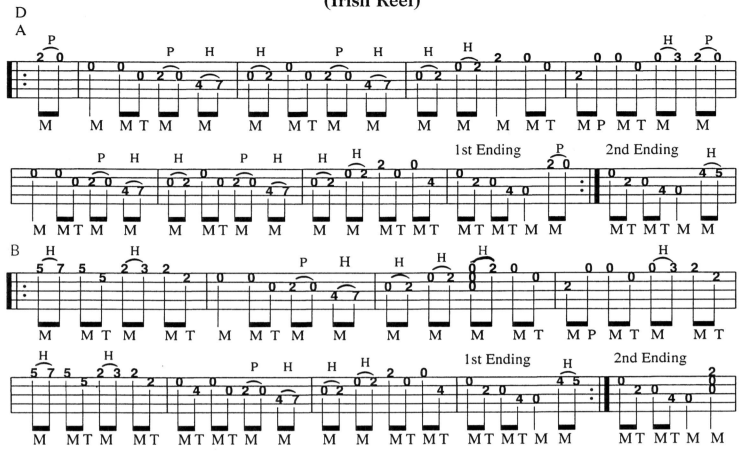

# LAMPLIGHTER'S REEL
## (New England Reel)

127

# ROAD TO LISDONVARNA
## (Irish Reel)

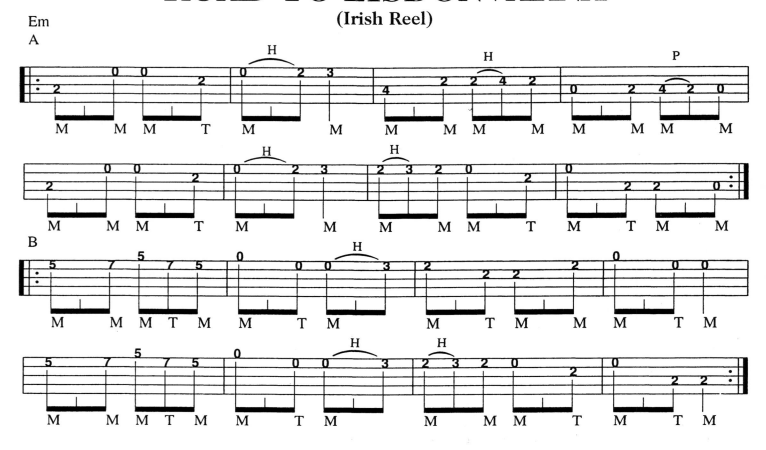

# THE MILL
## (Scottish)

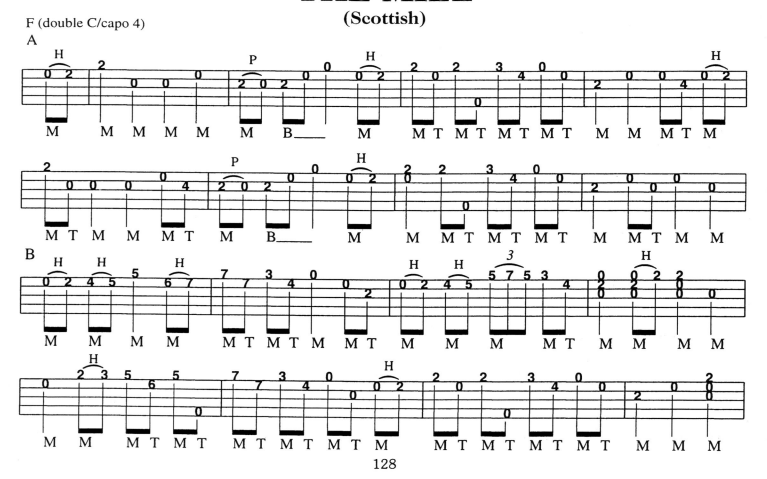

# ST. MARTINMAS TIME
## (Irish)

A

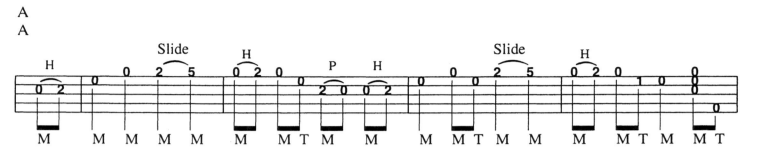

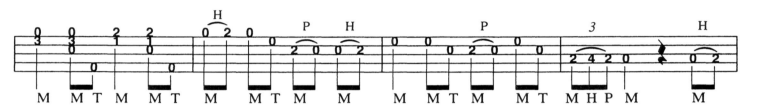

B

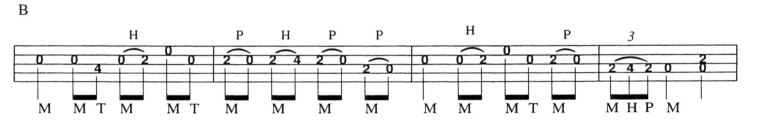

A1

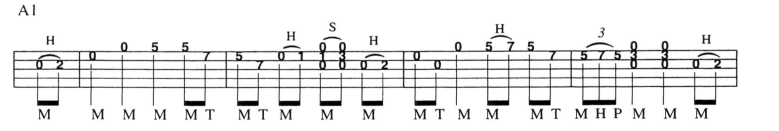

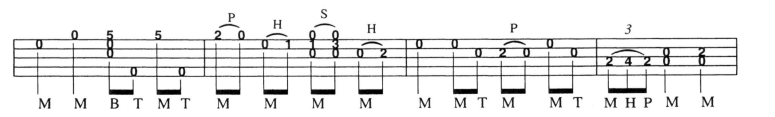

# LITTLE STACK OF WHEAT
### (Irish Hornpipe)

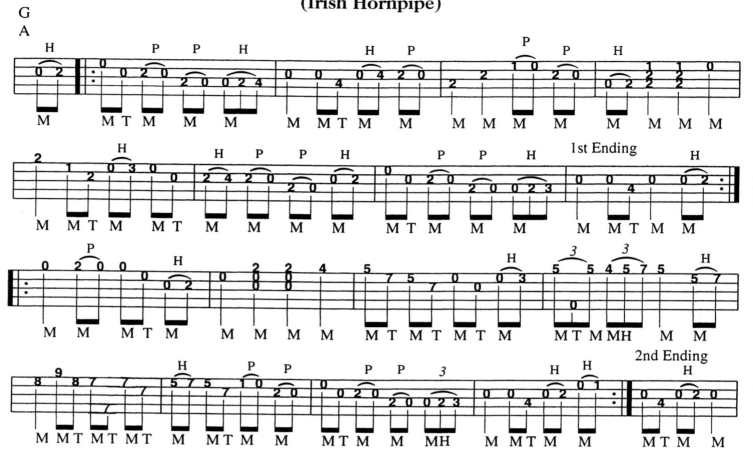

# P STANDS FOR PADDY
### (Irish)

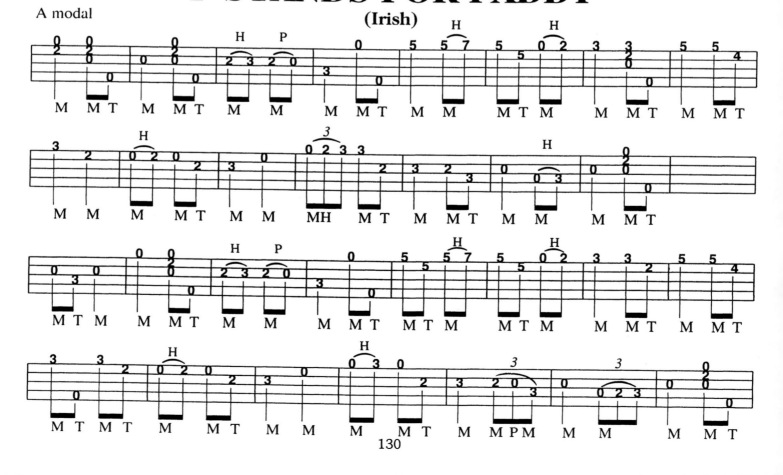

# SIEGE OF ENNIS

## (Scottish March)

D*
A

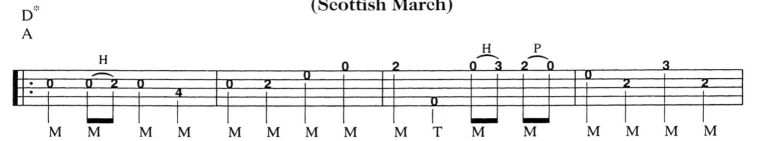

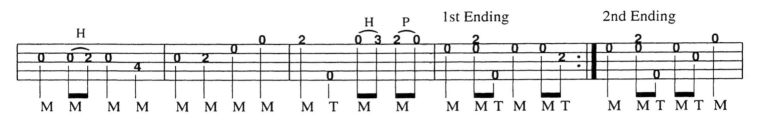

B

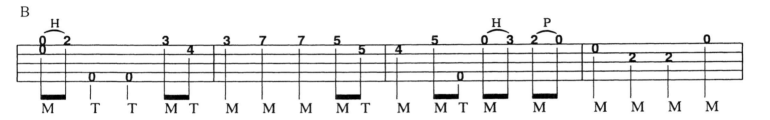

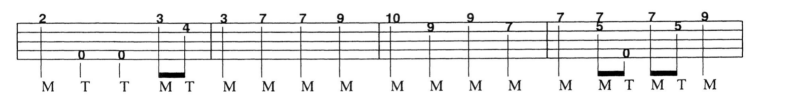

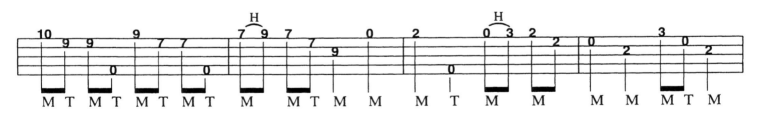

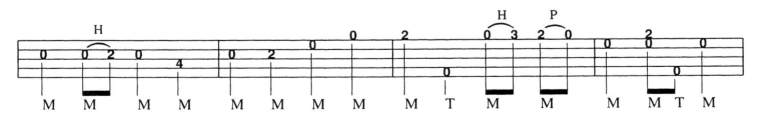

Traditionally Played in G

# WILLIE MOORE
## (American)

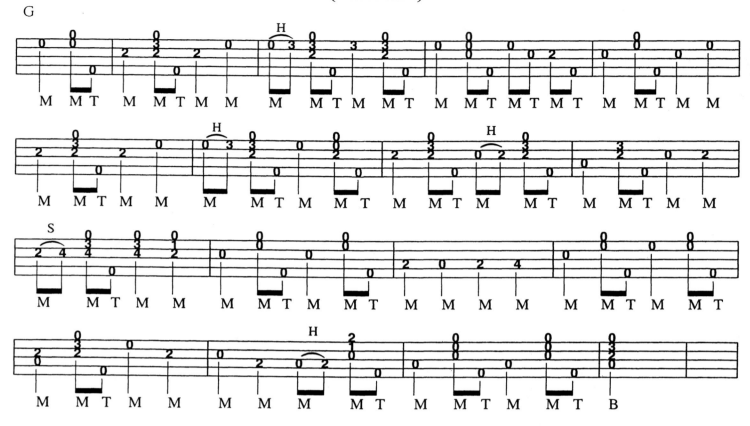

# ROAD TO BOSTON
## (New England)

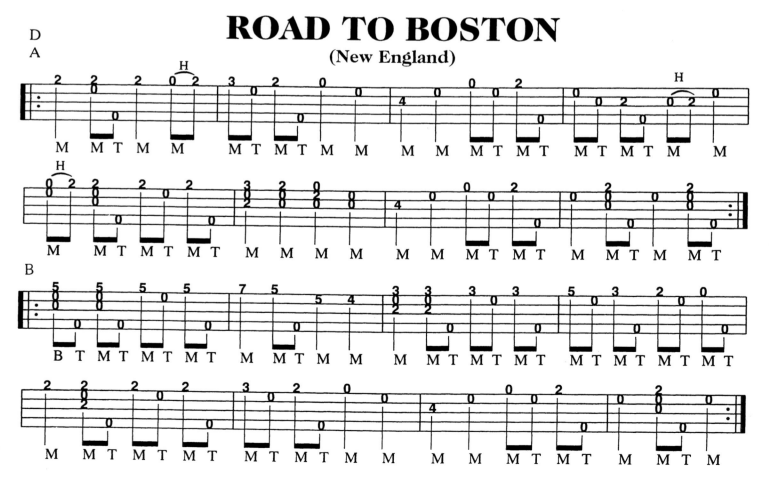

# YELLOW ROSE OF TEXAS

## (American)

D

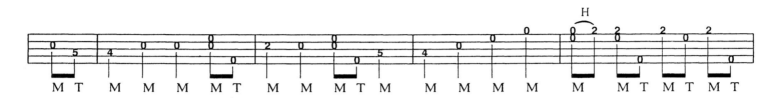

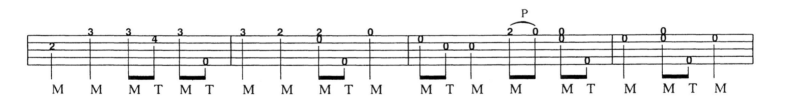

# TIKI TIKI LA
## (Cajun American)

# SIMPLE GIFTS
### (Shaker)

# GOD REST YE MERRY GENTLEMEN
### (English)

# BILLY MALLEY SCHOTTISHE

**(Scottish March)**

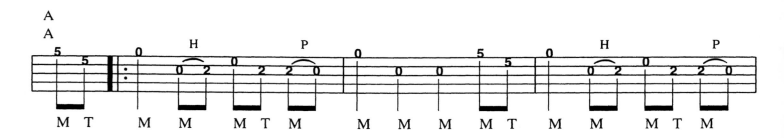

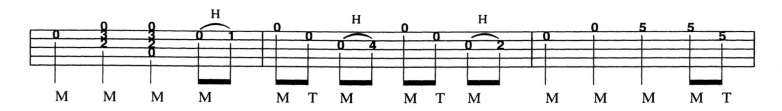

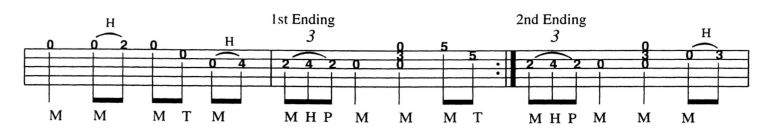

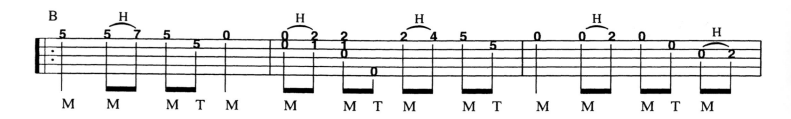

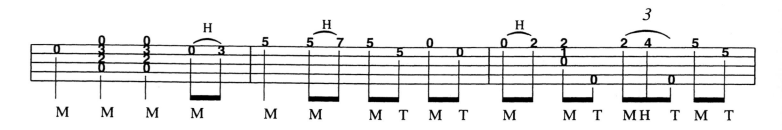

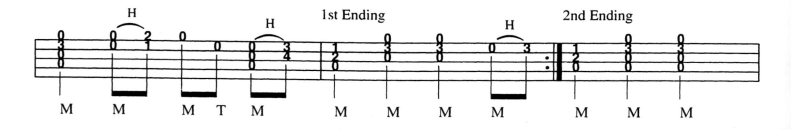

# THE GREEN MEADOWS REEL
## (Irish Reel)

# RECONCILIATION
## (Irish)

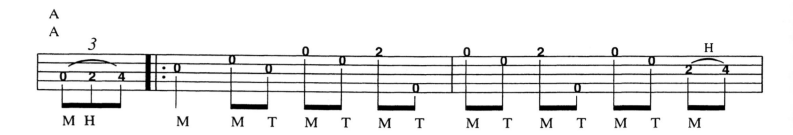

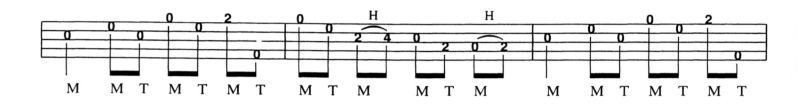

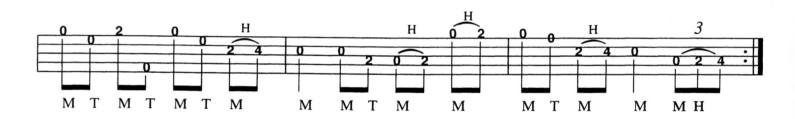

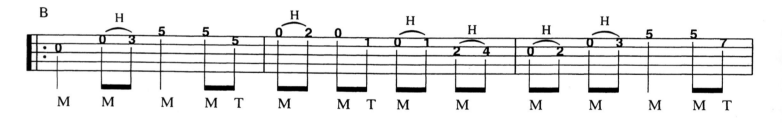

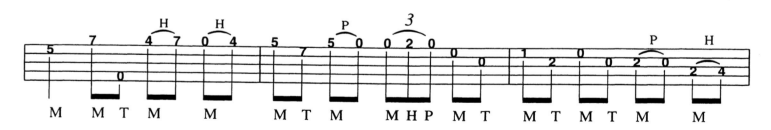

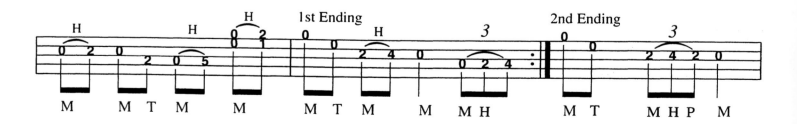

# THE FROST IS ALL OVER

### (Irish Jig)

# THE TOP OF CORK ROAD

## (Irish Jig)

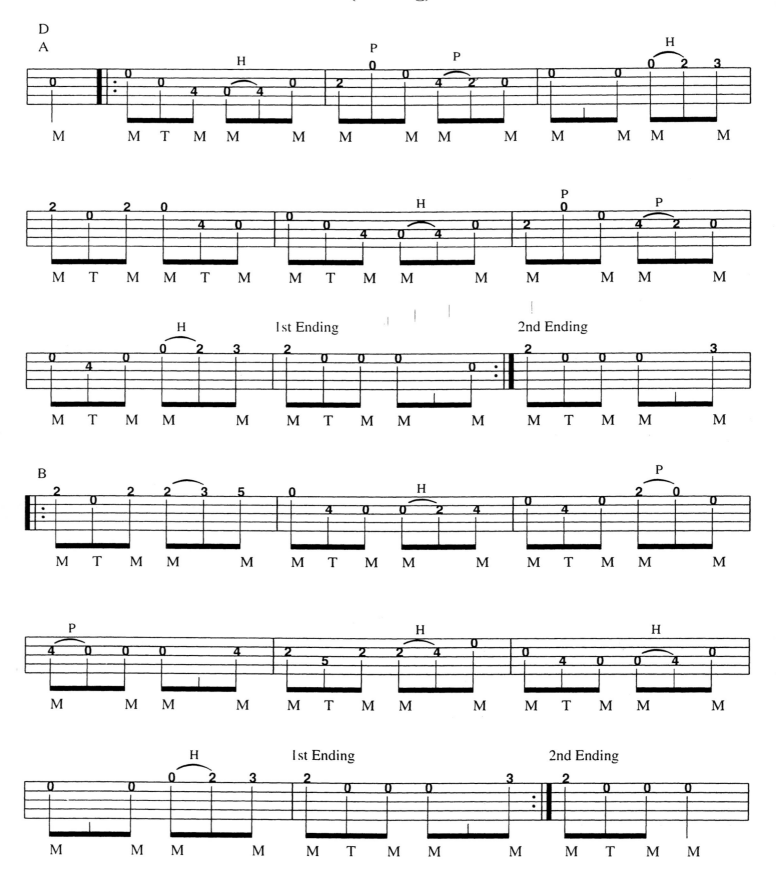

# FORKED DEER

## (Old-Time)

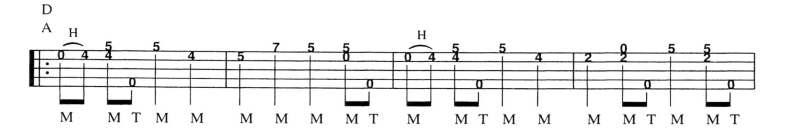

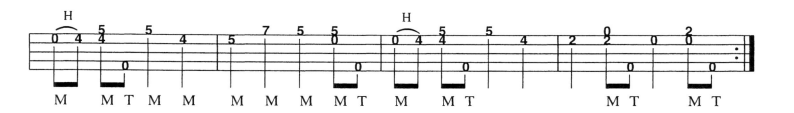

**B**

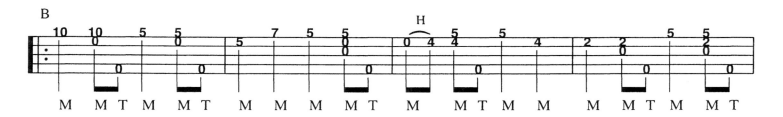

1st Ending

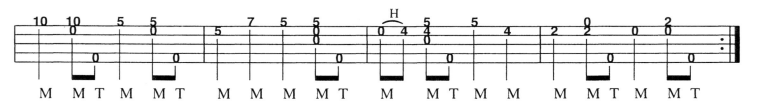

2nd Ending

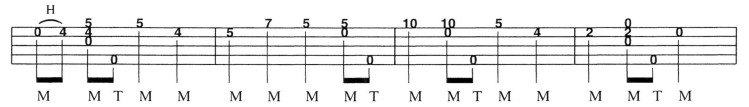

# THE HARE IN THE CORN

(Irish Jig)

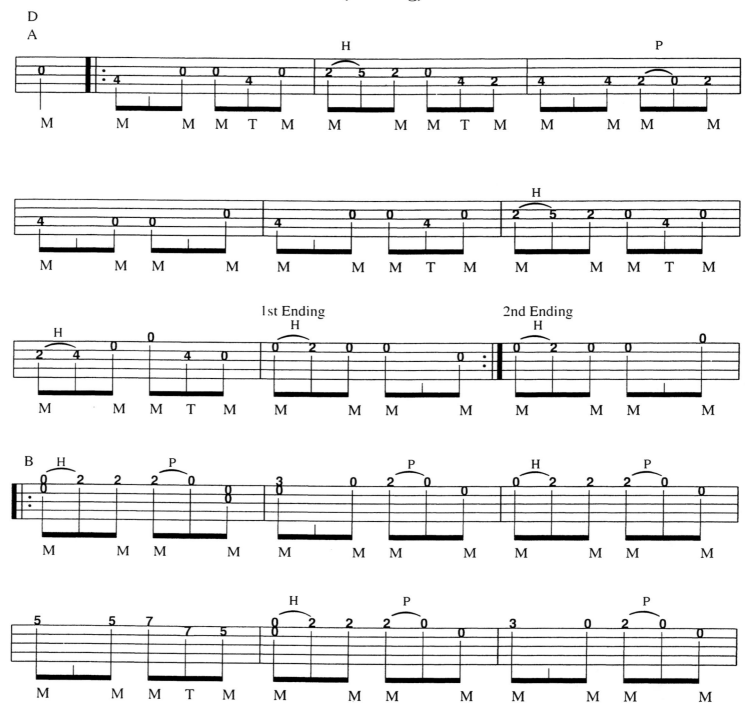

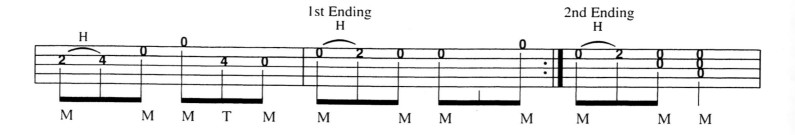

# BEHIND THE BUSH IN THE GARDEN

## (Irish Jig)

dbl C tuning
Am
A

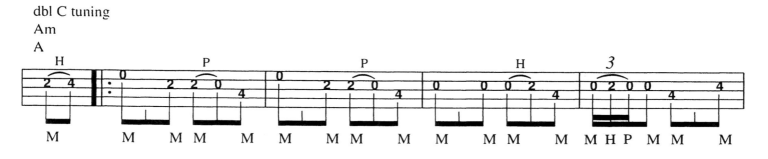

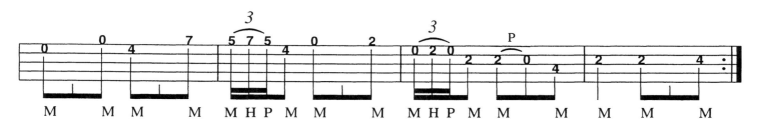

B

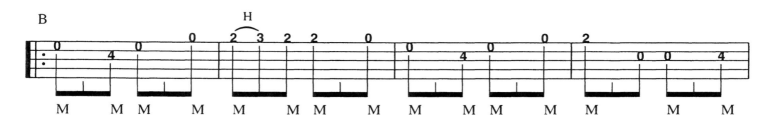

1st Ending

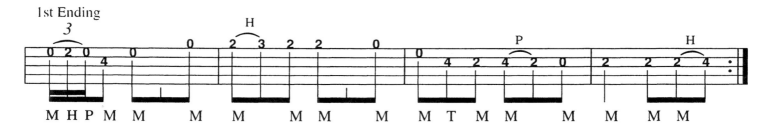

2nd Ending

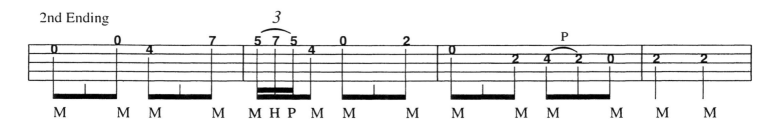

# DISCOGRAPHY

*The Bothy Band '75,* Green Linnet Records, New Canaan, CT, 1983.

*The Flowers of Edinburgh,* Laurie Riley, Bob McNally & Friends, Handcrafted Recordings, Hibernia, NJ, 1985.

*Cold Blow and the Rainy Night,* Planxty, Martin-Colter Music, Inc., 1974, P Shanachie Records, 1979.

*Andy Irvine/Paul Brady,* Green Linnet Records, 1981.

*The Gathering,* Greenhayes Recordings, Marketed by Flying Fish, Inc., Chicago, IL 1981.

*Heartdance,* Songs of the Wood Music, Black Mountain, NC 1986.

*The Woman I Loved So Well,* Planxty, Tara Records Ltd., Dublin, Ireland, 1980.

*Maloy,* Brady & Peoples, Mulligan, LUN 017.

*The Driven Bow,* Alasdair Fraser.

*Up Close,* Kevin Burke, Green Linnet Records, New Canaan, CT.

*St. Kilda Wedding,* Ossian, Iona Records, Glasgow, Scotland.

*To Welcome in the Spring,* John Roberts, Tony Barrand, Distributed by Elderly Catalog, Lansing, MI.

*New Englanders' Choice,* Skip Gorman, Folk Legacy Records, Inc., Sharon, CT, 1983.

*Martin Hayes,* Green Linnet Records, New Canaan, CT, 1993.

# BIBLIOGRAPHY

*Fiddler's Fake Book,* David Brody, Oak Publications, New York, NY, 1983.

*O'Neill—The Dance Music of Ireland,* Fodhla Printing, Dublin, Ireland.

*New Lost City Rambler's Songbook,* Mike Seeger, Tracy Schwartz, John Cohen, Oak Publications, New York, NY, 1964.